Post-Pandemic Pedagogy

Post-Pandemic Pedagogy

Tools of the TESOL Trade

A compendium of the Woosong University
TESOL-MALL Graduate Program/KOTESOL DCC
2021 Spring Symposium

Edited by

David Kent

KOTESOL
대한영어교육학회
KOTESOL DCC
Korea Teachers of English to Speakers of Other Languages
Daejeon-Chungcheong Chapter
https://koreatesol.org/daejeon

Daejeon, Republic of Korea.
대한민국 대전

First Edition.

DEDICATION

*For the students and alumni of the
TESOL-MALL graduate program at Woosong University,
and to all members of KOTESOL be they past, present, or future.*

CONTENTS

ACKNOWLEDGMENTS

I wish to extend my deepest appreciation to my wife *Hyunhee* who has been very patient and understanding throughout the entire process involved with the production of this book, and the instigation, coordination, and running of the associated symposium from which these chapters originate. It has certainly been a challenge to take another symposium from concept to fruition while essentially doing everything alone. There are many tasks from organizing a location, preparing it and the surrounds on the day, and organizing catering. To name a few others, there are, of course: arranging presenters, editing abstracts, preparing and editing a program book, designing artwork and ads for event promotion, as well as deciding on themes for the event, then promoting the event with posters and across social media, contacting presenters and those registered to attend, preparing lanyards, and presenter and attendee packets, securing certificates of presentation/attendance (posting these out if necessary), and obtaining prizes from organizations such as Oxford University Press, the transcoding of presentation videos, creating descriptions for them and hosting them across social media and YouTube, preparing and presenting any awards, as well as designing and preparing a website for the event along with collating, editing, cover designing, and printing any proceedings. Special thanks to *Mark Love* for finally moderating sessions on the day, to *Travis Frank*, *Ryan Hatcher*, and *Michael Peacock* for serving as best presentation judges, and to *Noel David* for serving as the tiebreaking judge. I would also like to thank *Michael Peacock* and KOTESOL DCC for lending their name and affiliating with the symposium, thereby helping both of us to fulfill the KOTESOL DCC and the TESOL-MALL graduate program aim of providing teacher education and professional development to the wider Daejeon community, the Republic of Korea, and the globe. As a lifetime member of KOTESOL I am pleased to be working on events such as this one.

PREFACE

Post-Pandemic Pedagogy

As teachers taught through the global pandemic that began in Asia during the later months of 2019, and has since gripped the world, they have employed technology and their training to lead educational change. They have achieved this by riding the wave of a paradigm shift for the mainstream provision of education, predominantly by rising to the challenge of adapting to and delivering emergency remote teaching. Changes moving forward will likely continue with the ever-increasing digitalization of education, the hybridization of education on return to the classroom, and the possible increase of blended and distance learning offerings institution-wide (along with an increasing need to develop asynchronous and synchronous online and offline learning activities and opportunities for learners).

Teaching today would not be possible without the onset of the fourth industrial revolution, which also brings with it many changes and challenges for educators (Kent, 2019). It is now impossible to teach students all of the content that they need to learn, and so emphasis needs to be placed on the need to teach our students aspects of 21st century skills, digital citizenship, and most importantly, those soft skills that will allow them to adapt and to change their approaches, their thinking, and their ways of implementing and completing any project that they approach, and the learning that they need to develop in order to perform any work or tasks required of them, or any hobbies that they may wish to enjoy. Learning these skillsets also sees students needing to engage with content in increasingly different ways to achieve their learning goals. For instructors, also, it may very well come to change with who we will teach, and how we might best need to begin the integration of AI-based content and assistants into our classrooms (Kent, 2020). So too, as language teachers, we need to understand that with this new phase of education comes a fundamental change in the nature of how we may begin to use the languages that we learn, and also why we may need to learn them, and this will also impact significantly on how we should be teaching them (Underwood, 2018). Essentially then, what is important to recognize at this stage is that what this disruption offers us as educators is an opportunity. It is a chance to reorient how we deliver instruction and reach our students, with it coming at a time where we must also rely heavily on our training to guide and teach our learners as we expand ourselves and expand our repertoire.

Rationale for the Text

This book puts forth a snapshot of how English as a foreign language (EFL) teachers in the Republic of Korea professionally handled the 'COVID crisis', and how they now see their craft, their administrative, teaching, and learning contexts, as well as how their learners should be educated in not only a post-pandemic, but possibly a COVID endemic world. It is therefore an essential read for any educator, student, administrator, or stakeholder involved with the teaching English to speakers of other languages (TESOL), particularly those who want to understand how pre-service and in-service teachers are honing their teaching craft, and how post-pandemic pedagogy is currently impacting the educational sector.

Chapters for the book emerge from those presentations delivered at the 2021 TESOL-MALL Graduate Program – KOTESOL DCC Symposium, held via Zoom session at Woosong University in Daejeon, Republic of Korea on May 29 of 2021. The event was host to a number of synchronous events, as well as a number of asynchronous pre-recorded sessions released in the lead up to the event. This book now serves as a record of the abstracts and the presentations delivered as part of this event, and stands as the third book in the symposium series.

Organization of the Text

The book consists of eight chapters, and it is intended to be read as a whole or in part by teachers, students, parents, professors, administrators, and any other stakeholders who may be interested in the topics. All chapters reflect a broad range of issues that surround the symposium theme, from that of building successful on-demand video courses, teaching successful test-taking strategies to learners, dynamic rubric development, to the integration of student generated content in courses, as well as those of leading social justice, communicating across cultural barriers, developing learner management system wiki use, and exploring evolving teacher-student identities in emergency remote teaching.

Wayne Finley, from Korea Polytechnic University, provides the opening chapter of the book, *building successful on-demand video courses*. In this dynamic and easy to read chapter, he defines what is meant by on-demand video course development and delivery through a MOOC (massive open online course) system such as Udemy. He details the basic equipment required for the development of such courses, before addressing the processes behind structuring, designing, shooting, editing, and the uploading of video. He closes by then discussing aspects of marketing such courses to a global student base.

Miranda Wu (Wu Yang), from Huaihua University in the People's Republic of China, and David Kent from Woosong University in the Republic of Korea, consider *working memory strategy efficacy for the Pearson Test of English Academic Speaking*. In their chapter they examine aspects of how to obtain better performance in the PTEA Academic test by exploring strategies and cognitive factors that influence test-taker performance.

Jan Mathys de Beer, from Woosong University, then provides chapter three, *time-saving dynamic rubrics for effective online feedback and scoring*, in which he details a practical hands-on example of how to convert a standard rubric into a dynamic rubric using

Microsoft Excel. The application and use of such a dynamic rubric can save time while also providing a means for easily giving effective personalized feedback to learners, and it is one that can be used across the gamut of online, hybrid, and face-to-face classroom settings.

In chapter four, Andrew Aguiar and Nicole Shiosaki, both of Gyeongsang National University, discuss how to approach the teaching of English as a foreign language through the development of *integrated approaches using student generated content*. The chapter specifically highlights how the use of student generated content can be applied through the use of Nation's four strands and an integrated approach when teaching, with a variety of practical examples that can be adapted or used directly being provided.

Cyril Reyes, of Woosong University, then argues passionately in *defense of social justice in education*, in chapter five. He explores this argument from three perspectives, detailing how teachers who identify with any of these camps can engage in social activism in their classroom and with their students if they so choose.

In chapter six, Retha Choi from Woosong Information College explores aspects of *communicating with students in the Korean classroom – crossing the cultural barrier (preconceptions and cultural differences)*. This chapter of the book highlights some of the classroom communication issues that may impact on foreign teachers who move to the Republic of Korea to teach, with the example discussed stemming from her 25-years of teaching on the peninsula.

Michael Cary of Kyonggi University – Suwon campus then provides a discussion regarding *university LMS-based wiki use with writing students during emergency remote teaching* from chapter seven. He details a range of LMS-based writing activities that he found useful to apply during emergency remote teaching, and those that student feedback shows they enjoyed.

Finally, Valentin Tassev of Woosong University, in the closing chapter of the book considers *evolving identities and teacher-student relationships in the midst of COVID-19*. As the subtitle, teacher notes, suggests, this chapter is a reflection on the change in students and the teacher when delivering emergency remote teaching in an audio only style. This is seen to be liberating for the Chinese students of EFL and the native-speaking English language teacher involved, and an experience that opened up new opportunities of academic development and engagement with the language under study.

Ultimately, this book series intends to provide both education and something new for all of those who are interested in the field of TESOL. I trust that it will leave you with a fresh understanding of what can be brought to the classroom when we, as educators, take into consideration the power of post-pandemic pedagogy and the tools of the TESOL trade.

David Kent, Ed.D.
Associate Professor/Head of Department
TESOL-MALL Graduate Program, Woosong University

References

Kent, D. (2020). A room with a VUI – Voice user interfaces in the TESOL classroom. *Teaching English with Technology Journal, 20*(3), 96-123.

Underwood, J. (2018). *Using voice and AI assistants for language learning*. British Council Teaching English Webinar. https://www.teachingenglish.org.uk/article/using-voice-ai-assistants-language-laerning

1. Building Successful On-Demand Video Courses

Wayne Finley
Korea Polytechnic University

Abstract

The coronavirus pandemic of 2020 thrust many teachers into the world of online teaching but teaching online is nothing new. Massive open online courses (MOOCs) available through providers like Udemy and Coursera have long proven to be extremely popular. As of today, Udemy has more than 40 million learners, 50,000 instructors and over 30 million minutes of on-demand content. The popularity of MOOCs offers a world of opportunity for teachers. Successful on-demand video courses reach thousands of students all over the globe and can generate a reliable source of passive income. This chapter will cover the basics of everything a teacher requires to build courses for commercial MOOC providers like Udemy. From acquiring the right equipment, structuring the curriculum, creating engaging content, through to editing of the videos and the means of launching a successful marketing campaign for the created course. You will finish this chapter receiving all the basics for building successful on-demand video courses, and what's more, you will also receive valuable tips and advice to give your courses the upper hand in such a competitive environment. MOOCs are here and they are here to stay. Read on to get started!

Introduction

Before the coronavirus pandemic catapulted education online in 2020, many teachers were already turning their attentions to the Internet. New platforms were emerging; platforms that appealed to the needs and wants of the modern learner. The on-demand learner. The learner who consumes education like they consume television on Netflix.

The educational landscape was changing before the pandemic hit, and it was only a matter of time before its transformation was complete. The lockdowns, and classroom lockouts, of 2020 accelerated the progression from bricks-and-mortar to webcams and microphones for many teachers forced to move to emergency remote teaching. Through 2021 and beyond, I envision that new skills will be required of all teachers: the skills to build successful on-demand video courses.

The Move to MOOCs

MOOCs (massive open online courses) are not new, but they have never been more popular. Coursera, one of the most well-known providers, was founded in 2012 by Andrew Ng and Daphne Koller, computer science professors at Stanford University in the U.S. At first the platform was just offered to their own students, but its growth potential was soon recognized, and thus it began its journey to what it is today. A platform partnered with at least 190 universities that boasted 40 million users (or 'learners') in 2019 (Sawers, 2019). It offers a wide variety of qualifications, including those of university degrees.

When a university requests on-demand video courses from their teachers, it is usually for the Coursera platform. However, while Coursera undoubtedly holds dominion over online university education, it does not hold a grip on online education in general. The power of the Internet is that it can potentially remove barriers and gatekeepers. Platforms like YouTube have allowed anyone with a creative idea, or a force of personality, to become stars (or 'influencers'). MOOC providers such as Udemy have enabled anyone to become educators. No official teaching qualifications or credentials required.

Udemy, in its current form, came into being in 2010 and within just a few months had 10,000 registered users (Toto, 2010). As of February 2021, it has 40 million (Udemy, 2021). The big selling point of Udemy is that it is 'The Academy of You'. Anyone is free to upload their courses as long as they pass Udemy's 'Quality Review Process', which looks at several factors, but the main ones are video/audio quality and potential for copyright infringement. Course content is judged not so much by Udemy, but by students who complete the courses via Udemy's public review system.

In the past, teachers' sole competition for income was other teachers who completed the same qualifications, and perhaps worked for the same employer or went for the same job position. While this concept still holds true to a certain extent with MOOC platforms like Coursera, it does not hold true with popular platforms like Udemy. The instructor with the most popular course(s) gains the most students and makes the most money. It does not matter if they have a PhD in Applied Linguistics from Oxford University or they went into the world of work at age 18 and have never developed a course prior. Fortunately for the teacher who has never built a successful on-demand video course, the skills required to do so can be developed relatively quickly.

Basic Equipment for Online Course Development
The basic tools of a bricks-and-mortar teacher's trade are perhaps a whiteboard, a few board markers and a textbook. The computer is a bonus; a chance to display a colorful PowerPoint, an image or a video through the projector. Additionally, to provide interactivity they may use apps and gamification to liven up their courses and provide learning using different modalities. However, for a teacher building on-demand video courses, a lot of those tools fall by the wayside. The possibilities for an on-demand video course teacher are many and a lot of decisions

have to be made over what equipment will be utilized, and this chapter will discuss this in more detail. Initial thoughts though, turn to the video camera; the means by which the teaching will be delivered.

Advances in technology mean that the majority of teachers already possess a video camera that is suitable for filming on-demand video courses, and this may very well be encapsulated within their smart phone. Any smart phone capable of recording video in high definition (upwards of 1080p) meets the expectations of most MOOC providers. In fact, Udemy limits video courses to a resolution of 720p, but permits 1080p if requested by the instructor. The only necessity for teachers is that they keep their cameras still, and this is usually achieved through use of a tripod. Some successful courses do not make use of a camera at all: the instructor speaks over PowerPoint slides or images and only their voice is heard. However, teachers of the most successful on-demand video courses show their faces on camera.

High quality video can easily be attained through a smart phone. The same cannot be said of what I consider the most important equipment factor in on-demand video courses: the microphone. A teacher can be forgiven for a blurry or out-of-focus-video, but clear audio is pivotal. The 'Quality Review Process' of Udemy, for example, places great emphasis on it. Any teacher wishing to build successful on-demand video courses should consider investing in a dedicated microphone. There are two kinds of microphones to choose from: a shotgun microphone and a lavalier microphone. The shotgun microphone stays in position, pointed at the teacher. The lavalier microphone is pin-sized and can be worn by the teacher.

When deciding on the type of microphone to invest in, teachers should consider their environment and the needs of their course. If the teacher plans to speak from one static position, for example a desk or a podium, then a shotgun microphone will suffice, as long as the recording environment contains little echo. If the teacher plans to move and speak, perhaps around a room or demonstration area, then a lavalier microphone will prove to be the better choice. The audio level stays consistent. A lavalier microphone is also a better choice for recording environments likely to suffer from echo, such as small rooms with wooden flooring. Teachers, however, are not expected to have studio-quality sound in their on-demand video courses. As long as the audio is clear, audible and consistent, there will be few complaints from students, and it will likely pass the standards of on-demand course providers.

Another option for teachers to consider is a chroma key background, the most popular of which is a green screen. The benefit of a chroma key background is that it transports teachers out of their environment and places them anywhere of their choosing. If, for example, an English Language teacher wants to cover food vocabulary, they can change their backdrop to that of a restaurant or a food store. If it's a lesson on geographical features, the teacher can look as though they're standing atop a volcano or deep under the ocean exploring the Mariana Trench. Some on-demand video course instructors opt to have static chroma key backgrounds, such as solid white or gradient blue. It can look more professional than a natural setting, such as a teacher's apartment or office.

Poor lighting is one mistake that teachers make on their first forays into filming video. Lighting is something taken for granted in face-to-face teaching: teachers hit the classroom light switch and they have all the light they'll ever need. Not so in on-demand video teaching. Great efforts are made in videography to capture the right amount of light. Teachers should check how the lighting looks on film. Filming outdoors in the daytime, or just making sure the filming environment is brightly light, is enough for most teachers. For the more dedicated videographers, there are other options. One budget option is softbox lighting: two studio lights, usually out of sight of the camera, facing the teacher. Softbox lights are affordable and available through most major marketplace websites, such as Coupang or Gmarket in the Republic of Korea (hereafter Korea) or Amazon globally. They bring soft, even light to every video.

The two most basic technological requirements of preparing on-demand video courses are that of the video camera and the microphone, and aside from lighting, there is one more consideration that all teachers soon discover: video editing. The most popular hardware for running editing software today are desktop computers and laptops. Most come with enough horsepower (CPU, GPU and RAM) to run software that can perform basic video editing tasks (e.g., editing short videos up to a resolution of 1080p). More advanced video editing, such as wanting to apply digital effects and to edit in resolutions up to 4K, require more powerful computers. One option for teachers on a budget, though, is video editing on a smart phone or tablet: there are a number of apps such as LumaFusion that perform almost all of the same tasks available to users of basic computer-based software. For now, and prior to discussing aspects of shooting, editing and uploading video for an on-demand course, consideration needs to be placed on structuring the course and then the course design.

Structuring the Course
The traditional structure of face-to-face university classes in Korea is usually one semester of 15 weeks, with one or two classes each week. Each class may be two hours in length with one 10-minute break in the middle and one at the end. On-demand video courses are very different. A lot of popular courses on Udemy, for example, are just a few hours in length. A whole

course may be consumed in just one sitting. Classes, in the traditional sense, do not exist. On-demand video courses have sections, and each section contains several video clips. The student is free to drop in and drop out as they see fit. Attendance is at their discretion. If their first impression of the course is poor, company policies like Udemy's refund policy allows students to withdraw and receive a full refund within the first 30 days of their course purchase.

From my perspective, successful on-demand video course instructors do not forget the tenets of traditional course design, but adapt them. Every course taught in a classroom can conceivably then be adapted to work in and on-demand video course. A mistake that some teachers may make is not adapting: they try to teach in exactly the same way as they normally would, but with a camera in front of them. The video filmed then may end up being one long lecture without any thought given to the adapting to use of the new medium. All the interactivity and dynamism of a face-to-face class is potentially lost. The solution for structuring an on-demand video course is simple: keep the videos short, make them engaging and use some form of interaction.

The total length of the course can vary. One popular language course on Udemy is the 'English for Beginners: Intensive Spoken English Course', which takes 77 hours to complete. Another popular course, 'English Grammar – Tenses and Verb Structures' takes only 1.5 hours to complete. Both courses are sold for almost the same price. The longer course is 17,000 Korean won (~$17 US dollars), and the shorter course is 15,000 (~$15 US dollars). However, it does appear that students see more value for money in longer courses. From these examples, the longer course currently has 37,174 students and the shorter course 8,304 students. This trend appears to hold true across most categories on the Udemy platform.

While the length of on-demand video courses may vary, the highest-rated courses tend to share one characteristic: videos range from two to twenty-five minutes in length. Most are in the range of three to ten minutes. Udemy itself recommends videos between two to six minutes. There could be a few reasons for that rationale. Students studying through computer screens may find it more difficult to concentrate. Unlike a face-to-face course, teacher talk time is not complemented with ample student talk time. Perhaps also, there is an expectation that on-demand video courses should provide a variety of short video clips, similar to that people consume across other platforms such as YouTube, or those that may appear in a social media feed.

In a face-to-face class, student engagement is important, but on a platform like Udemy, it is pivotal. Teachers need to share useful content, but they need to do so in an as engaging manner as possible. Students can leave reviews for courses after watching just one video. In most cases, that is just a few minutes after enrollment. If the teacher does not grab the student's attention and engage them immediately, they may find themselves with a poor review. Consequently, potential future students may be discouraged from enrolling in the on-demand video course based on that single review. The successful on-demand video course educator must become an engaging video communicator.

The communication skills required of an on-demand video course developer/teacher are similar to those of a teacher in the classroom, but there are some adjustments that are required. First, all successful teachers, whether being filmed for a video or presenting a lesson in a classroom, must possess an ability to teach the content and material that they are providing in a manner that students can engage with and potentially learn from. There are a number of ways for a teacher to do this. For example, they can choose materials suitable for the level of the students. They can adapt materials and communicate concepts through varying methods of instruction. In a face-to-face class, the teacher can also learn, through trial-and-error, what works best with the students that are in front of them.

In an on-demand video course, there is no adapting to the students in real time, as the class is asynchronous. Interaction, if any, may only consist of a 'thank you for enrolling' and a 'thank you for completing the course' message. The on-demand video teacher then needs to choose a level before creating the course and adhere to it throughout, just as would normally be done in a face-to-face course. If students feel the level too high, or too low, there is no reward for them, and if targeted correctly they will know the level is wrong for them. On a university campus, some students may rejoice at an easier-than-expected class. A chance for an 'easy A'. Not so on commercial MOOC platforms like Udemy. While some students are primarily motivated by course completion certificates, they do however expect to learn and improve upon the skills they possess. They can only do that through appropriate leveling, and the understanding of what this means for them when they enroll. When creating a course, Udemy offers four options: beginner, intermediate, expert and all levels.

Effective communicators in the classroom command attention. Through their voice, body language, gestures and overall presence, students know when it is time to listen to instructions, complete activities and receive feedback. When sharing concepts, telling stories or presenting information, communication skills demand interest. There is no monotone voice. Arms are not folded. The classroom looks like the exact place that communicator/teacher wants to be. They display a clear passion and focus for teaching. If a teacher's communication skills are ineffective in the classroom, then this will come across more so on video.

The video medium magnifies communication skills. There is no hiding place on screen. In a classroom, a language teacher with less-than-stellar communication skills could achieve a successful career through other facets of great teaching: lesson planning, varied instruction, maximal student talk time. On video, the teacher is front and center. The star of the show. To be successful, the teacher should speaker clearly. If to a beginner level, then adjusting speed and vocabulary just as in the face-to-face classroom. Vocal tone should be varied and show enthusiasm. Concepts should be presented clearly and visually. Eye contact should be made with the camera and the teacher should look comfortable with the camera.

In order to build rapport with students they will never meet, most successful video teachers appear on camera. Their face is visible and expressive. Some teachers take it a step further and show themselves from the waist up. This is a good strategy. It allows the teacher to use gestures and body language to illustrate points and display warmth in their communication. The teacher is either permanently on camera with the visuals to the side (e.g., the Microsoft PowerPoint), or they cut between themselves and the visuals. Another method successful on-demand video teachers use is to speak conversationally, as though they were tutoring, and teaching a one-on-one class.

Course Design

After attaining the equipment and building confidence in their communication skills, and having structured the course, the next step is to design the on-demand video course and prepare the materials. Unlike a face-to-face course where a teacher may create a syllabus and then prepare materials class by class, all materials should be ready before the first day of shooting video. It allows the teacher to see the big picture and record the videos efficiently. If everything is prepared prior, an on-demand video course can be shot quickly. Some on-demand video teachers shoot all of their content in one day. Others, over a few days or a week. However, if the teacher does not know exactly what they are filming and needs to create materials between each shoot, then the total time to complete the course could be much higher.

There are a number of options for visuals in on-demand video courses. The easiest is, perhaps, to use a Microsoft PowerPoint presentation for each video. These are easy to create and, if the teacher is doing screen recordings with their face automatically superimposed in the corner, quick to produce. The teacher may also opt to show videos clips from websites like YouTube or, if they are conscious of copyright infringement, websites like Pixabay and Pexels. Do note that copyright is important to adhere as there is potential to be sued if using or broadcasting content without permission from the creator, even citing a program name incorrectly may lead to such an issue. That aside, animation is also a popular choice; there are many applications available to quickly design high quality drawings, such as PowToon and Vyond, which allow use of content for commercial purposes (such as in on-demand video courses). If teachers want to go the route of making explainer videos, ones that look like they show their hand drawing on a canvas, then VideoScribe and MySimpleShow could be good choices.

A lot of successful on-demand video teachers also design interactive materials and plan for them in their on-demand videos. For example, an on-demand video course can be designed to include time for students to complete worksheets. On-demand videos do not only have to be lectures. At the beginning of the course, the teacher can instruct students to download the worksheets they have created for use with each on-demand video. At the right time in the on-demand video, the teacher relays instructions and displays a timer on the screen. Students may be given 5-10 minutes to then complete the associated worksheet before the teacher then goes through the answers on screen. Such interactivity, just as in a face-to-face classroom, can potentially deepen learning and perhaps also serve to maintain student focus.

Most MOOCs also offer students the opportunity to complete quizzes and assignments, and many on-demand video teachers take up this opportunity. The quizzes are automatically scored based on the correct answers that the teacher has provided the system. Such quizzes in an on-demand language learning video course may be best suited to grammatical exercises or listening tests. However, a number of on-demand video teachers do offer assignments that they will take the time to grade. It can be a unique selling point for their course and drive students to enroll in their on-demand video course over that of a competitor's. It can also give a boost in student ratings: one category students review Udemy instructors on is if they have 'helpful practice activities'. Taking the time to create quizzes and assignments to complement any on-demand video course could then pay dividends.

One question would-be on-demand video teachers may have is whether they should write scripts. One benefit of writing a script for each video to be recorded, is that it allows clear organization of thought and clarity of speech. However, the teacher may sound more like a narrator of a documentary than a teacher in a classroom. Another benefit though, is that the creation of scripts allows for subtitles to be uploaded quickly and without errors. There is no reliance on auto-generated subtitles, which the teacher has to comb through for mistakes manually. However, while there are these benefits, the general consensus is against scriptwriting. In a physical classroom, few, if any, teachers prepare scripts/lectures for language teaching. The result is speech that sounds natural, authentic and perhaps more likely to connect with students. Another advantage is that course completion time is much faster: scripts generally take a considerable amount of time to draft and redraft.

Shooting Video
Teachers should test their filming locations before engaging in any actual video shooting for the courses they intend to provide on-demand. They need to film a test shoot to access acoustics, check lighting, adjust camera focus and ensure that the area on camera is free of distractions. A good idea is to shoot test footage again and again until the image looks and feels right to you. If all of the materials are prepared, shooting the on-demand video elements can be one of the fastest parts of the whole course development project. An on-demand video course can be completed almost as fast as teaching a course in real time. The only delays in the filming of video might be unexpected equipment issues and outtakes. If the recorded video clips contain few, or no, mistakes or errors then it cuts down on the video editing time significantly. There is no need to edit out mispronunciations, unwanted pauses or other communication mistakes or errors.

Video Editing
As with Hollywood movie productions, the time spent editing video is significantly longer than the time spent on recording it. The exact amount of time depends on the skills of the video editor, how much editing is required and how straightforward the editing is. A lot of teachers new to recording on-demand video courses may choose to start with free video editing software. For owners of Apple computers, this choice might be iMovie: it is designed to run smoothly on their system, and it performs many of the basic video editing tasks that will be required in on-demand video course production. For Windows users, the choice is more difficult: teachers have to search for

free software as Microsoft MovieMaker has long been removed from the system. A quick search shows numerous applications claiming to be free, but they often possess one limitation or another and thus making them unsuitable for continued use. It may only be free during a trial period, the resolution of the final video may be limited, or the final video may contain a prominent watermark advertising the application.

For best results, paid software is often the most viable option. Final Cut Pro and Adobe Premiere Pro are the standout applications on MacOS. Adobe Premiere Pro is also available on Windows, as are other popular paid applications like DaVinci Resolve and Wondershare Filmora. Teachers should experiment and decide what software system works best for them. To produce a successful on-demand video course, only basic video editing is required. A cheaper application like Wondershare Filmora, or a free one like iMovie, will be more than sufficient. If, however, teachers want to produce videos that stand out among the competition, they may wish to invest in one of the paid options available to them. They should also gain access to laptop or desktop computer proven to be good for video editing projects. If they are not sure, though, a safe choice may be that of Apple computer: they come bundled with free creative software that is tailormade to work on the system.

Uploading

When a teacher has finished editing their on-demand video clips, it is time to then go about uploading them to the MOOC platform of their choice. Most of these platforms make it a simple process. Udemy, for example, allows the option of uploading videos individually or in bulk. The bulk option is best; uploading can take several hours to complete, depending on connection speeds, and so it is advised to leave the on-demand videos uploading overnight. After upload of the on-demand videos, it is then time to sort them. Sections need to be named. The on-demand videos need to be titled. Supplementary materials need to be attached. The course once was just an idea in the teacher's mind, and outlined in a document or piece of paper during the structuring and design phase, but is now given existence in digital form. As with any upload of digital content, it is wise for the teacher to check that all of content, including the on-demand videos have been uploaded correctly, and that everything appears as desired.

Marketing

Once the on-demand video course is uploaded, some would say the real work begins. No matter how good the on-demand video course is, it will not be successful without marketing. Time must be spent on creating an engaging course landing page that persuades potential students to enroll in the course. The Udemy course landing page consists of the course title, course subtitle, course image, preview video, a 'what you'll learn' box, a list of course requirements, the course description and the instructor profile/bio. To rise to the top of the Udemy search results and gain attention, teachers might wish to look over the course landing pages of the best-selling courses. They serve as a great model and will show that the course landing page is as much a selling point/advertisement as it is a description of the on-demand video course contents.

Some MOOC providers do not advertise on-demand video courses for the teachers on their platform, and there is no real ecosystem for students to discover it organically. Other MOOCs like Udemy are online catalogues: students click on categories and search for the on-demand courses that they have an interest in pursuing. If a course is performing well in the number of student enrollments, it will rise to the top of these search results. One popular method for new teachers to raise publicity is to offer course coupons. On Udemy, the teacher is free to offer their course completely free for a set time period of three days. If then promoted on a variety of social media platforms, then this could lead to lots of enrollments very quickly. There are a number of Facebook groups, for example, for teachers to begin to share their free coupons. Other promotional offers could be discounted prices. For example, offering the on-demand video course at a cost of 15,000 Korean won (~$15 US dollars) for one month.

Conclusion

There is a world of opportunity for teachers to build on-demand video courses for popular commercial MOOCs like Udemy. To be successful at such an endeavor all teachers need do is acquire the tools, adapt their skills and develop sound marketing strategies for their course(s). The equipment needed is affordable and easily obtainable. The skills, most experienced teachers already have, and it is just a matter of adapting them. The marketing side may be new to a lot of teachers, but a lot of useful and effective advice can be gained quickly through the strategic use of search engines. There has never been a better time for teachers to build successful on-demand video courses. Start today!

References

Sawers, P. (2019, April 25). *Coursera raises $103 million to prepare online learners for the 'fourth industrial revolution'*. Venture Beat. https://venturebeat.com/2019/04/25/coursera-raises-103-million-to-prepare-online-learners-for-the-fourth-industrial-revolution/

Toto, S. (2010). *How Coursera makes money*. Investopedia. https://www.investopedia.com/articles/investing/042815/how-coursera-works-makes-money.asp#:~:text=Its%20base%20of%20users%2C%20who,%2465.48%20billion%20worldwide%20by%202026.

Udemy. (2021). *Improving lives through learning*. Udemy, Inc. https://about.udemy.com

Useful Links
Adobe Premiere Pro
https://www.adobe.com/products/premiere.html
Coupang https://www.coupang.com
Coursera https://www.coursera.org
DaVinci Resolve
https://www.blackmagicdesign.com/products/davinciresolve
Final Cut Pro https://www.apple.com/final-cut-pro
Gmarket https://www.gmarket.co.kr
iMovie https://www.apple.com/imovie
LumaFusion https://luma-touch.com/lumafusion-for-ios-2
MySimpleShow https://www.mysimpleshow.com
Pexels https://www.pexels.com
Pixabay https://pixabay.com
PowToon https://www.powtoon.com
Udemy https://www.udemy.com
VideoScribe https://www.videoscribe.co/en
Vyond https://www.vyond.com
Wondershare Filmora https://filmora.wondershare.com

2. Working Memory Strategy Efficacy for the Pearson Test of English Academic Speaking

Miranda Wu (Wu Yang)
Huaihua University

David Kent
Woosong University

Abstract

In the computer-based Pearson Test of English Academic (PTEA), test-takers and instructors are usually eager to understand how the reporting algorithm is based on the enabling skills (ES) and communicative skills (CS) scores shown on test reports. Undoubtedly, their interest in investigating the algorithm is driven by endeavoring how to develop strategies to improve their speaking score. This chapter examines aspects of how to obtain better performance in this test, by exploring strategies and cognitive factors that influence test-taker performance, analyzing 214 score reports collected from 107 participants over a treatment period of three-year years. Findings from three experiments show that working memory (WM) strategies can explain significant variance in complexity, accuracy and fluency (CAF) for test-takers. Fluency, reflected by articulation speed, breakdowns and repair, is the predominant component here because the use of fluency-oriented strategies can improve speaking performance rapidly and lead to lexical complexity and phonological accuracy transfer. Cognitive factors such as response latency, speed fluency, attention, confidence and target score as motivation are also significant for such variance. This illustrates the importance of mapping learners' meta-cognition with WM strategies during instruction to optimize their test outcome, which has implications for tutors assisting students in achieving their desired PTEA target score.

Introduction

Working memory (WM) has been substantially studied in terms of general capacity and brain plasticity (Lilienthal et al., 2013; McNamara & Scott, 2001) using laboratory or online digit, letter, words or object stimulus tasks as memory span tests (Burgess & Hitch, 1999; Daneman & Carpenter, 1980). However, less exploration of WM training efficacy from a semantic level has been undertaken (e.g., the use of sentence-level or lecture-level tasks within L2 language assessment contexts). The five tasks of Read Aloud (RA), Repeat Sentence (RS), Describe Image (DI), Retell Lecture (RL) and Answer Short Question (ASQ) in PTEA speaking are measured at such a level that require cognitive listening comprehension and speech production to occur. Few studies have examined the sentence level and task-based cognitive modalities of comprehension and production (Baese-Berk & Samuel, 2016). A competitive relationship between comprehension and production is suggested with the inherent urge of production and cognitive demands possibly modulating the relationship, as suggest by Gavens and Barrouillet (2004). Other scholars view listening and speaking as bilateral accounts (e.g., Clark and Krych, 2004) which form an integrated activity instead of being autonomous (Ferreira, 2000; Levelt, 1989) in the cognitive process.

The PTEA reports scores of around 70 speaking tasks based on 6 enabling skills including oral fluency, pronunciation, vocabulary, written discourse, spelling and grammar (Zheng & de Jong, 2011). Despite being told that the tasks are measured integrally among the various communicative skills of listening, speaking, reading and writing, it is hard for test-takers to develop task-based strategies to improve performance.

Moreover, this style of test interpretation and linguistic construct from score reporting make it difficult but necessary to see variance emerge based upon the individual's prior knowledge and background, personality, strategies in test-taking, characteristics and general cognitive ability (Messick, 1995; Housen & Simoens, 2016).

Granena (2019) found cognitive factors influential for L2 learning, especially in WM training for speaking proficiency. The impact of working memory on L2 learning may not be straightforward if only considering linguistic factors (Freed et al., 2017), or when other latent cognitive variables like processing speed, IQ and knowledge, language experience are not considered (Sakai, 2018). In addition, most studies observe WM training outcomes from self-generated independent-task designs (Wei & Zheng, 2017) rather than the transfer of WM as an acquired cognitive skill for broader verbal tasks (Gathercole et al., 2019). Driven by the integral task design nature and the proprietary reporting algorithm in PTEA, the study explores WM strategies and develops sub-constructs for experiment efficacy from a linguistic-cognitive perspective with an aim to improve test-takers' speaking scores by trading off among complexity, accuracy and fluency (CAF).

Research Questions

In this study, the following questions are addressed:

1. Are working memory strategy constructs effective for answering PTEA speaking items?
2. Are cognitive factors influential in explaining variances in speaking performance for those sitting the PTEA?

Literature Review

Speaking Performance Facets: Linguistic CAF and Cognitive Constructs

Although the CAF framework of syntactic complexity, grammatical accuracy and fluency have established measurement standards for linguistic research for more than two decades, it has faced criticisms by scholars regarding the questionable validity of latent construct representation (Pallotti 2009) when applied to different tasks (Lambert & Kormos, 2014). Housen, Kuiken and Vedder (2012) proposed a multi-componential model for L2 performance and investigated its linguistic subcomponents with cognitive dimensions. Vercellotti (2017) studied the development of CAF as subcomponents and in terms of being the ultimate objective of second language development. Some studies tested the trade-offs in L2 learning taking into account both linguistic and cognitive variables (Skehan, 2009; Robinson, 2003, 2011), while Granena (2019) investigated the underlying constructs of cognitive aptitudes of speaking proficiency using language aptitude batteries loaded on factors of explicit aptitude, and implicit ability such as memory.

Alternatively, De Jong et al. (2012) examined the facets of second-language (L2) speaking performance with a model that included 9 linguistic knowledge and processing predictors, including: vocabulary, grammar, lexical retrieval speed, speed of articulation in response latency, duration, speed of building sentences, pronunciation of sounds, intonation and word stress. Prior to this, other models, such as Higgs and Clifford's relative contribution model (1982) stated that the increased weight in linguistic knowledge or speed of processing predicts a higher gain in speaking proficiency. Zahedi and Shamsaee (2012) explored skill integration, a manner of both language and information manipulating skills as a synthetic operation in internet-based language testing in terms of the PTEA relying on integrated tasks. Zheng and de Jong (2011) explained test-takers' prior linguistic knowledge and general cognitive ability and illustrate how this can influence reporting scores.

Moreover, other researchers, such as Xie and Dong (2017) found that language experience, more specifically, bilingualism (in terms of L2 verbal fluency) and public speaking experience, incur enhancement in aspects of cognitive control. Ren (2014) used retrospective verbal reports to longitudinally examine how higher level L2 learners involved in the cognitive processes involved with the completion of multimedia tasks undertaken in the English language, during their study abroad, show that affective variables such as motivation, self-confidence, L2 speaking anxiety in virtual cultural experiences, risk-taking and grit in and out of class influence L2 speaking ability (see also Lee & Lee, 2019). Grimshaw and Cardoso (2018) investigated in class activities for promoting speaking fluency and found that anxiety effect and willingness to communicate can be meditated by virtual gameplay and task-specific language activities. They also found that self-confidence was found to explain achievement in oral communication in trained interactional sessions, which was positively impacted by interactional strategies for information gap tasks. Other affective factors like learners' enjoyment and willingness to communicate were found to decrease over time, but self-confidence was significantly enhanced by training (Van Batenburg et al., 2019). Munezane (2015) investigated the relative cognitive effects of visualization and target settings, which were found to have a positive influence on L2 speaking fluency and content.

In brief, this listing of researchers indicates that scholars are interpreting linguistic CAF in a variety of ways, and as a result cognitive factors in task-based scenarios lead to a wide variety of findings.

Task-Based Mnemonic Strategies

Ellis and Yuan (2004) found that task-based planning created a positive effect on improving CAF in narrative writing. Hsu (2017) studied task planning effects on L2 development in synchronous text-based and computer-mediated communication, seeing free recall in relation with experimental design moderated by differences in task materials and retrieval practice success rates, structure, length and when in presence of feedback (Mulligan et al., 2016).

Lambert and Kormos (2014) studied how CAF can be operationalized in task-based research by suggesting approaches to establish relevant measures for L2 performance. Taking this a step further, other research investigated the association between mnemonic non-verbal measures (i.e., fluid reasoning and visual processing intelligence) and the structure of WM using an episodic buffer (Gray et al., 2017). Other studies on the benefits of testing for enhancing episodic memory (Pan et al., 2015; Akan et al.,2018) despite individual differences (Robey, 2019), show possible proactive interference (Öztekin, & McElree, 2007) as well as influences from prior knowledge when conducting incremental associative learning (Bein et al., 2019). Phonological loop and visuospatial sketchpad models were proposed by Baddeley (1986), and in such WM models as relying on mnemonic strategies to reinforce rehearsal effects, improvement in visualization for episodic memory occured. Other phonological loop effects studies include those that were able to determine associations with vocabulary learning (Gupta & Tisdale, 2009), those on noun class learning competing with effects of semantic cues (Culbertson et al., 2017), those involving language disorders in children (Gathercole & Baddeley, 1990), as well as others on speech representation (Cowan et al., 1985), and adult speech production (Dabrowska, 2008).

In short, taken together, most studies found that using a combination of mnemonics to develop cognitive skills is constantly effective in providing better performance at a linguistic level.

Methods

Participant Profile and Treatment
Profile

A longitudinal study involving 107 participants (see table 1), providing PTEA score reports before and after training, and involving three experiments and online training sessions, was conducted over a period of 36 months (from February of 2018 through to January of 2021). The mean age of participants was 28.14 (SD = 7.82, range 16–54). A total of 214 PTEA score reports were collected from the participants, one before and one after involvement in the study. Prior PTEA scores indicate that all participants were unable to meet the sufficient score criteria for study in a foreign university or for immigration purposes, which usually requires an overall target score above that of 65, 79 or 86.

Table 1.

Participant profile

Variables	N	Range	Min	Max	Mean	SD
Age	107	38	16	54	28.14	7.82
Years spent learning English	107	39	1	40	17.21	7.47
Target score	107	21	65	86	74.88	7.32
Times taking the PTEA	107	9	1	10	2.15	1.44

Treatment

Treatment involved participants attending one-to-one online training sessions involving task-based speaking reinforcement practice based on PTEA tasks. Each treatment session lasted 2 hours, with 1 session held per day over a period of 14 days per training period. The one-to-one training sessions were provided via Zoom sessions, this allowed for audio-visual interaction between the instructor (one of the researchers) and participants, relying on a shared screen and a chat room for note-taking. Participants were also expected to work with the provided study materials between sessions, and practice the techniques introduced during each session in self-regulated learning practice.

Treatment also involved participants engaging in three experiments to explore the efficacy of task-based WM strategies through a read aloud (RA) experiment, a repeat sentence – answer short question (RS-ASQ) experiment, and a describe image (DI) and retell lecture (RL) experiment. While results are explored and discussed independently for these experiments, a paired participant t-test involving PTEA test scores for participants pre- and post-treatment was utilized to determine the efficacy of WM strategy use during treatment, across experiments, and to see if treatment sessions led to improving participant PTEA test scores.

Experiment Material and Apparatus

Material selected for use in treatment was sampled from simulation tests and include read aloud, repeat sentence, describe image, retell lecture, and answer short question practice tasks found in the PTEA. These kinds of tasks are incorporated into a variety of free mobile applications and websites[*]. A number of these also include aspects of artificial intelligence (AI) speech recognition and automatic evaluation technologies to

---

[*] For example, https://www.apeuni.com, and https://pte-ai.com/; https://www.ytaxx.com

support those learners who are attempting the PTEA speaking section. During treatment the use of these applications and websites were replied upon, and further supplemented with sentences and podcasts from Pearson (2010) and the Foreign Language Press (2016). In addition, real-time news from the BBC World Service was also utilized for note-taking purposes and retell lecture practice using a mobile application during treatment. Further, two American native English speakers were employed (out of 26 candidates) to record prompts for the experiments to test AI perception reliability and computer-generated speech synthesis technology maturity, upon which adjustment of the AI automatic reporting algorithm used by the mobile applications could be calibrated, and in turn then reliably used to rate participant pronunciation and fluency. These audio prompts were also provided to participants as demonstration answers and utilized as prompts during treatment for participants to imitate. A total of 2,024 prompts were recorded for various tasks found within the PTEA, including those of read aloud ($N = 303$), repeat sentence ($N = 623$), describe image ($N = 468$), retell lecture ($N = 138$), and answer short question ($N = 492$).

Study design

A quasi-experimental design was adopted in order to answer the research questions. Research question one was answered by conducting a paired samples t-test, to determine if treatment would provide a change in PTEA test score among participants. This, along with the overall results of the three experiments conducted and provided during treatment, was then taken into account in order to answer research question two and to determine if cognitive factors can explain working memory (WM) training variance.

Instruments
Pre-Treatment Survey
A perception survey based on constructs related to investigating participants prior knowledge of the English language, their perception of the PTEA, their motivation toward studying for the PTEA, and to ask participants their PTEA target score was delivered pre-treatment. The survey consist of 24 items, 9 open-ended and 15-closed ended. A survey link was distributed to participants, and they completed it anonymously through the Wenjuan platform (https://www.wenjuan.com/s/fI3AVr).

Treatment Experiments
The read aloud (RA), repeat sentence – answer short question (RS-ASQ) and describe image-retell lecture (DI-RL) experiments were conducted over the course of treatment and involve aspects of the use of complexity, accuracy, and fluency (CAF) constructs, AI-based pronunciation and oral fluency ranking of participants, as well as taking into consideration the tasks, traits, and score contributions and timings as found in the PTEA. Analysis was undertaken by SPSS for correlation and variance (ANOVA) for the CAF constructs during experiments, and treatment effect size comparing the dichotomous scores were analyzed by
JASP for an independent t-test.

Tasks, Traits, Score Contributions and Timings in the PTEA. Table 2 describes the tasks, traits, score contribution and timing found in the PTEA. Traits scored in speaking include that of content, oral fluency and pronunciation. In terms of the answer short question section, responses are either correct or incorrect depending on appropriateness and accuracy (Pearson, 2012). A 5-scale pronunciation rating scale is also employed by the test with 5 native-like, followed by 4 as advanced, 3 as good, 2 as intermediate, 1 as intrusive and 0 as non-English. Oral fluency scales are similar with 5 as native-like, 4 as advanced, 3 as good,

2 as intermediate, 1 as limited, and 0 as disfluent. As a result of this, content is rated differently, albeit in a similar fashion, across each of the three task-based experiments due to the variance found in the PTEA speaking test design.

Complexity, Accuracy, and Fluency (CAF) Constructs. Latent complexity, accuracy, and fluency (CAF) constructs, and coefficients indicating a better speaking score were investigated from the experiments. Strategies for cognitive production and comprehension processes include those of utilizing a phonological loop, employing episodic memory skills using visual-spatial sketchpad templates and note-taking. For better understanding and sense-making in retelling tasks, we used L1 interpretation and write from dictation (WFD) for RL and ASQ tasks during second experiment. Table 3 shows time allocated for these tasks during and after each 2-hour treatment session.

CAF constructs were measured with pauses and errors in total number and duration and across nine sub-constructs. These nine sub-constructs are:

1. *Speed fluency.* This is measured as articulation rate, or the overall speed of delivery for each prompt computed in the study using mean number of words spoken per second, divided by total phonation time (i.e., total speech duration excluding pauses).

2. *Breakdown fluency errors.* This refers to mid-clause pauses are unfilled pauses within clauses of given prompts with a duration more than 150 milliseconds, including errors of improper chunking of sense groups; between-clause pauses are unfilled pauses between clauses, with a duration of more than 250 milliseconds (Bosker et al, 2013); and filled pauses include those pauses using for example, 'ah', and 'eh'.

Table 2.

PTEA Speaking Items

Tasks	Traits	Score Contribution		Prompt Length	Timing
Read aloud (RA)	A text appears on screen. Read the text aloud	Overall Score		Text up to 60 words	Varies by item, depends on text length
		CS scores	Reading Speaking		
		ES scores	Pronunciation Oral Fluency		
Repeat sentence (RS)	After listening to a sentence, repeat the sentence	Overall Score		3 - 9 seconds	15 seconds
		CS scores	Listening Speaking		
		ES scores	Pronunciation Oral Fluency		
Describe image (DI)	An image appears on screen. Describe the image in detail	Overall Score		N/A	40 seconds
		CS scores	Reading Speaking		
		ES scores	Pronunciation Oral Fluency		
Retell lecture (RL)	After listening to or watching a lecture, retell the lecture in your own words	Overall Score		Up to 90 seconds	40 seconds
		CS scores	Reading Speaking		
		ES scores	Pronunciation Oral Fluency		
Answer short question (ASQ)	After listening to a question, answer with a single word or a few words	Overall Score		3 - 9 seconds	10 seconds
		CS scores	Listening Speaking		
		ES score	Vocabulary		

Table 3.

Task and Time Allocation During and After each Training Session

Item	During Session Minutes on Task	Number of Session Tasks	Post-Session Minutes on Task	Number of Self-Regulated Study Tasks	Total Tasks Undertaken
Read aloud	24	7	36	15	308
Repeat sentence	30	12	30	45	798
Describe image	30	7	30	30	518
Retell lecture	24	3	36	7	140
Answer short question	12	12	12	24	504
Total	120	41	144	121	2268

Note: Materials are PTEA practice items from Apps and websites; Visuospatial sketchpad and episodic buffer practice are applied for RS and RL practice using BBC real time news.

3. *Repair fluency errors.* These dysfluencies include repetitions, reformulations, false starts, and self-corrections per speech (< = 40 seconds).
4. *Pronunciation errors.* These are segmental errors, meaning phonemic substitutions, syllable structure errors (i.e., number of vowel and consonant insertion and deletion errors) and word stress errors, and these re highlighted in red and black during evaluation of speech using AI.
5. *Rhythm combo.* This refers to the correct pronunciation for all marked chunking, assimilation and deletion speech acts produced by participants (i.e., reduced or weakened syllables by linking and plosion, and the correct sentence emphasis and intonation used for paralleling and interrogative sentence structures in a marked RA prompt).
6. *Repeat sentence (RS) combo.* Successive recall of 3 sentences in correct word count, order and form within 3 seconds response latency, without fluency errors.
7. *Write for dictation (WFD) combo.* Continuous dictation of 3 short sentences (or short questions of 8 to 20 words) within 3 seconds response latency in absolute correctness (words are in correct form and order).
8. *Describe image (DI) combo.* Three consecutive described images without obvious detected breakdown and repair fluency errors including filled pauses using for example, eh, ah; unfilled pauses (duration more than 250 milliseconds) mid and between clauses; and repetitions, false starts, hesitations and self-corrections.
9. *RL combo.* A combo for RL is measured from every completion of a four-step assignment for BBC real time news retelling and summarizing spoken text practice including shadowing (phonological loop), retelling with notes and templates.

AI-Based Pronunciation and Oral Fluency Perception. Tavakoli and Skehan (2005) investigated three sub-constructs specifically related to fluency: a) breakdown fluency, concerning frequency, duration and location of pauses at sentence level; b) speed fluency in reference to the speed of sentence delivery; and c) repair fluency as repetitions, reformulations, self-corrections and false starts. These fluency sub-constructs were utilized in combination with an application-based AI pronunciation and oral fluency measure of participant speech production across each experiment. AI perception, using a mobile application, was based on a 90-point scale for both pronunciation and oral fluency.

Experiments Results and Discussion

Experiment 1: Read Aloud (RA)

According to the pre-treatment survey data, 16 participants (15%) regarded read aloud as the most difficult task in speaking because they conserved their pronunciation poor. Most of the participants feared that new vocabulary would hinder their chunking and interfere with being able to speak at a natural pace. To determine if this is the case, read aloud activities are the focus of experiment one.

Design and Procedures

In this experiment the investigation considers whether participants can chunk words into meaningful groups and read with a natural pace and fluency (meaning speed fluency as in articulation rate; breakdown fluency as in mid and final cause pause rate and duration; and repair fluency as measured by dysfluency rate, see Gathercole & Baddeley, 1990; Tavakoli & Skehan, 2005; Suzuki & Kormos, 2019), and whether or not they can read with correct pronunciation (measured in word stress, sentence emphasis and intonation measured as rhythm error rate), and whether or not they need to practice from phonic rules for consonants and vowels sounds (measured as syllable structure error rate). Here, content is an error-count measure for each replacement, omission or insertion of a word. Strategies based on participants' recordings were developed by quantifying (practicing to avoid) errors in each prompt aiming to improve participants' linguistic proficiency and confidence using the designated application. The practice of inputting speech sounds to a computer before the test in this experiment also allowed participants to practice adjusting their volume, and speech speed and in identifying when it is that they pause. In this phonological loop drill, participants were expected to imitate native English speaker recorded prompts to assist in their development of a standard L2 pronunciation, rhythm, and speech chunking.

During treatment sessions, participant errors in pronunciation were recorded and corrected in terms of pronunciation and breakdown fluency (including those of repetition, self-correction, reformulation and false starts). Participants were encouraged during the session, and to continue practice at home, in articulating their speech faster, moderating their volume and performing chunking until they reached a specific target score using the designated application for practice. Table 4 shows the descriptive statistics for CAF measurements, the aspects of AI automated assessed pronunciation and the oral fluency emerging among participants during the read aloud experiment.

Table 4.

Statistics of CAF Measurements and AI Perception for the RA Experiment

Measures	N	Min	Max	Mean	SD
AI Perceived Pronunciation	107	10.00	90.00	52.28	23.30
AI Perceived Fluency	107	10.00	90.00	66.05	20.88
Speed Fluency	107	1.82	2.24	2.02	0.16
Breakdown Fluency Errors	107	80.00	200.00	126.59	42.60
Repair Fluency Errors	107	47.00	100.00	75.69	13.03
Pronunciation Errors	107	100.00	460.00	168.64	66.09

RA Experiment Results and Discussion

Firstly, a correlation between articulation rate (the speed of overall delivery measured as speed fluency) and AI perceived fluency ($r = 0.515$) was observed. Speed fluency also positively correlated with post-training fluency scores on the participants' PTEA reports (measured as fluency 2, $r = 0.767$), see table 5. Moreover, 56% of the breakdown fluency errors in mid-clause pauses were linked and plosion related. Assimilation and deletion of sounds in a continuous and relatively fast speech is an important characteristic of being native-like (Pearson, 2011). The proprietary PTEA application used for AI evaluation of participant work marked words in red that were not recognized by it, marked words in black that it weakly recognized, and marked words in green that it considered correct in terms of pronunciation and fluency.

Secondly, the higher the speed fluency or articulation rate is, then the higher the oral fluency score will be, and in turn the overall speaking score also improves. This indicates that there is a trade-off effect between speed fluency and pronunciation. Articulation speed is the most important predictor for automatically assessed read aloud performance. Perceived fluency and listener-based comprehensibility (by both human and AI) are commonly associated with linguistic constructs of pronunciation and breakdown fluency (also proved by Suzuki & Kormos, 2019). This experiment provides further evidence for the correlation of AI perceived fluency and speed fluency, i.e., the faster overall speed of human delivery of a read aloud can possibly predict a better AI-based fluency score. As can be seen from Table 5, the frequency of mid-clause pauses (breakdown fluency errors) tremendously influences oral fluency in a negative way (r = -0.938). Lastly, repair fluency errors are significantly correlated with speed fluency (r = -0.854), and post-treatment speaking performance scores (r = -0.767), which provides implications for strategies in terms of read aloud training needing to avoid repetition, reformulation, self-correction and false starts, and participants reading aloud with correct chunking, word stress, linking and plosion, sentence emphasis and intonation.

Experiment 2: Repeat Sentence – Answer Short Question (RS-ASQ)

According to the pre-treatment survey, 50 participants (46.7%) revealed that the PTEA repeat sentence task was one of the most challenging because they were not able to remember what was said (n = 58, 54.2%), and figure 1. Limited working memory capacity (Baddeley, 2000) and the pressure of speaking under timed conditions (n = 25, 23.4%) were also perceived as reasons for seeing this PTEA task as challenging. Answer short question tasks were also perceived to be the challenging items for participants (n = 5, 4.7%) because they consider them difficult to comprehend due to the nature of the questions and as a result of an inadequate vocabulary scope. For this reason, these two specific tasks became the focus of the second experiment.

Table 5.

AI Perceived and RA-CAF Measurements Correlation

	Fluency 2	Speed Fluency	Speaking 2	Breakdown Fluency Errors	Repair Fluency Errors	AI Perceived Pronunciation	AI Perceived Fluency	Pronunciation Errors
Fluency 2	1	0.767**	0.893**	-0.583**	-0.840**	0.541**	0.631**	-0.649**
Speed Fluency	0.767**	1	0.715**	-0.492**	-0.854**	0.417**	0.515**	-0.493**
Speaking 2	0.893**	0.715**	1	-0.620**	-0.767**	0.602**	0.664**	-0.734**
Breakdown Fluency Errors	-0.583**	-0.492**	-0.620**	1	0.524**	-0.746**	-0.938**	0.581**
Repair Fluency Errors	-0.840**	-0.854**	-0.767**	0.524**	1	-0.483**	-0.536**	0.512**
AI Perceived Pronunciation	0.541**	0.417**	0.602**	-0.746**	-0.483**	1	0.780**	-0.640**
AI Perceived Fluency	0.631**	0.515**	0.664**	-0.938**	-0.536**	0.780**	1	-0.642**
Pronunciation Errors	-0.649**	-0.493**	-.734**	0.581**	0.512**	-0.640**	-0.642**	1

Note: P ≤ 0.01

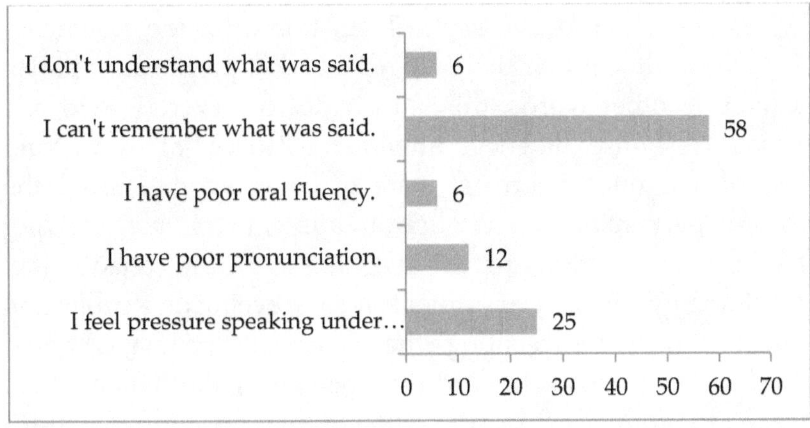

Figure 1. *Why I Feel the PTEA Repeat Sentence Task Challenging*

Design and Procedures

Techniques of rehearsal (Peng & Fuchs, 2017), episodic buffering (Robey, 2019), S1 interpretation (McManus & Marsden, 2017), note-taking and dictation (Onaha, 2004) were applied to mediate between production and comprehension in the repeat sentence – answer short question experiment. Short sentence recall and dictation combos (three successive correct sentences) were measured, with participants needing to recall and write down sentences using the correct form and applying correct word order and doing so with 3 second latency. In each case, participants practiced with a single native English speaker prompt, as an audio track, for a five-minute period. They were able to practice with one track of short sentences in each one-to-one session and utilize a different track during self-regulated at home practice. This practice involved a four-step process consisting of various mnemonic drills involving a phonological loop drill, an episodic buffer drill, and L1 transfer with interpretation drill, and an answer short question – write for dictation drill.

Step one: Phonological loop drill. In this drill, the researcher plays the audio and participants repeat what they hear in parrot fashion. In other words, this is a shadowing exercise with a 1 second response latency intended. Pauses of any kind (breakdown fluency errors) were to be avoided. During the process, participants were taught to apply a strategy involving the use of a visuospatial sketchpad during shadowing, imagining typing on a computer screen or seeing on a projection screen an image representing what they hear (one imaged typed word or image for each word that they hear). Participants then needed to group these words or images into meaningful chunks based on the rhythm of the audio. The intent here results from shadowing exercises being carried out with a purpose of imitating the speaker's pronunciation and intonation, practicing being idiomatic in use of expressions, relaxing oral muscles in order to help obtain increased proficiency in articulation and utilizing short-term memory to achieve sentence comprehension.

Step one: Episodic buffer drill. An episodic buffer drill has the intent of applying a method where active listening helps to enhance working memory efficacy by associating pictures and scenarios in the brain based on key words that are comprehensible to the listener when audio is played. In this drill the researcher plays the audio prompt a second time, and participants repeat the sentence. At the end of the sentence, there will be a pause to record participants' performance. The researcher made a note as to when each participant was able to correctly recall the sentence. If participants were able to successfully recall 3 sentences in a row this was termed a 'RS combo' and used in data analysis.

Step three: L1 transfer with interpretation drill. In this drill the researcher plays the audio prompt for a third time and participants interpret the sentence in their first language. The researcher then verifies the participants understanding of the sentence by how they have responded using L1 output, a method proven to be effective in L2 comprehension and production (see McManus & Marsden, 2017; Samuel & Larraza, 2015; Cox, 2017).

Step four: Answer short question – write for dictation drill. In this drill the audio is played, and the participants the write down the sentence. They are supposed to focus on accuracy (e.g., word order, spelling, form) while also focusing on answering the question. A record of each correct response was noted by the researcher with 3 continuously correct responses designated an 'ASQ-WFD combo' and used in data analysis.

Repeat Sentence – Answer Short Question Experiment Results and Discussion

In this experiment participants made 39,688 errors in total for pronunciation and fluency, both human detected and AI perceived. Pronunciation errors (*Sum* = 18044, *M* = 168.64, *SD* = 66.09), breakdown fluency errors of mid-clause, between-clause filled and unfilled pauses (*Sum* = 13545, *M* = 126.59, *SD* = 42.60) and repair fluency errors of repetition, hesitation, self-correction and reformulation (*Sum* = 8099, *M* = 75.69, *SD* = 13.03). These statistics are reflected in table 6.

Table 1.

Descriptive Statistics of Participant Errors in the Repeat Sentence – Answer Short Question Experiment

Error Type	N	Mean	SD	Sum
Pronunciation	107	168.64	66.09	18044
Breakdown Fluency	107	126.59	42.6	13545
Repair Fluency	107	75.69	13.03	8099

On further investigation, a strong negative correlation was found between experimental errors and pronunciation (r = -0.900). The relationship between repair fluency errors and fluency score is also significant at the 0.01 level with r = -0.840. The breakdown fluency errors and post-treatment fluency rates correlated at r = -0.583. We observed that repair fluency error is more negatively correlated with the post-treatment fluency score than the breakdown error score, indicating that although participants are prone to pause and hesitate during their recall of short sentences for repeat sentence and answer short question tasks, with the behavior of breakdowns (repetitions, false starts and reformulations) having a more devastating impact on oral fluency score (see Table 7).

Table 7.

Correlations Among Pronunciation and Fluency Measures in the Repeat Sentence – Answer Short Question Experiment

Measures	Post-Training Pronunciation	Post-Training Fluency
Breakdown Fluency Errors	-0.581**	-0.583**
Repair Fluency Errors	-0.555**	-0.840**
Pronunciation Errors	-0.900**	-0.649**

Note: P ≤ 0.01

Control of attention and anxiety are essential deciders of participant breakdown fluency. When undertaking step one: phonological loop drill, participants' focus should be a parrot-style shadowing exercise without any distracting or placing much attention on comprehension. Rather, with step two, they were encouraged to buffer episodically with the words flashing on an imaginary screen or a sketchpad before starting to then recall the sentence during an at ease state. In this step an immediate response from less than 1 to 3 seconds latency, due to the limits of human short-term memory capacity and duration (Hughes et al, 2016), was expected and would also be expected during actual test conditions. It was determined that response latency of longer than 3 seconds would impair accuracy and fluency scores significantly in recall, increasing lexical and grammatical complexity which results in failures of achieving what were designated an RS combo and an ASQ-WFD combo. Most participants casually reported to the researcher that the step one: phonological loop and the step two: episodic drill manage to divert attention from an immediate response after around 7 sessions of employing the four-step process of mnemonic drills. Some participants would later mention that having completed these drills alleviated their anxiety when sitting the actual test. Also, in step three: L1 transfer with interpretation drill the researcher encouraged participants to express what they comprehend in L!, and found that successful interpretation appeared to build confidence and proficiency in terms of achieving 'RS combo' scores and 'ASQ-WFD combo' scores. Of note also, the higher the pre-determined participant PTEA test target score, the more 'RS combo' and 'WFD combo' streaks they were able to accomplish. Further, ANOVA results show linearity between participant desired PTEA test target scores and their 'RS combo' score (significant at the 0.000 level, r = 0.377), with a linear correlation between the 'ASQ-WFD combo' score and the participant desired PTEA test target scores also significant at the 0.000 level (r = 0.296).

Experiment Three: Describe Image and Retell Lecture (DI-RL)
Design and Procedures

For the describe image and retell lecture experiment the describe image tasks involved showing an image to participants from a computer screen for 40 seconds. The images were maps, pictures, charts, tables, histograms, flowcharts, and pie charts. Some images were presented with word prompts (e.g., labels on a chart), and these were helpful for participants in terms of helping them produce basic sentence patterns and in alleviating breakdowns and repair fluency errors (especially if they had limited vocabulary to express what the image represents, Derwing et al., 2004). A pre-designed template used as a physical 'visuospatial sketchpad' (Ellis & Yuan, 2004, Camos et al, 2009; Sakai, 2018) was applied for participants to practice with while undertaking the tasks involved in this experiment. Unprepared participants were often observed to panic during a random occurrence of an image under timed conditions (describing 7 images continuously, with 25 seconds for viewing/planning and then 40 seconds for describing the image before the next would appear). Others showed lack of confidence when describing images and when balancing complexity, accuracy and fluency (CAF).

In the retell lecture tasks component of the experiment participants were expected to watch a short lecture (60-90 seconds worth of audio or video) and then retell it within 40 seconds. Templates provided for participants to use during this task were designed to achieve moderate complexity, accuracy, and fluency (CAF) using fixed and easy sentence structures. The aim was to help guarantee participant syntactic and semantic accuracy, along with decent lexical complexity and maximum fluency, because proficient sentence patterns allow the brain to allocate more attention to noting down key nominal phrases and logic conjunctions for accurate understanding. Along with the templates, a note-taking drill combined with L1 interpretation strategies were applied.

In the note taking drill participants were asked to use notes as memory aids with the compound use of symbols, abbreviations, and acronyms. Participants were encouraged to divide an A4 paper into small sections and take notes vertically, using a line feed technique for each sentence. L1 interpretation strategies involved focus and attention placed on noting functional words and logic markers, as well as nouns and nominal phrases particularly, because these largely decide whether participants can comprehend the lecture or not. Participants were expected to finish 7 retell lecture tasks using a three-step practice relying on real-time news from the BBC World Service that they were able to access via a mobile application in each one-to-one session. The three-step practice involved the notetaking drill, retelling of the lecture recording within 40 seconds, and making use of the templates to provide a written 70 ward maximum summary of the spoken text.

DI- RL Results and Discussion

Results from the ANOVA and the compared means show that both of the describe image and retell lecture combos are associated with speed fluency (overall speed of delivery). They are also positively correlated with fluency reported by participants when undertaking the actual PTEA test. Table 8 shows the strong association between describe image (DI) and retell lecture (RL) combos as well as speed fluency (DI combo*Speed fluency Eta = 0.964, RL Combo*Speed Fluency Eta = 0.981).

Table 8.

Measures of Association

Measures of Association	R	R Squared	Eta	Eta Squared
DI Combos * Speed Fluency	0.926	0.857	0.964	0.929
RL Combos * Speed Fluency	0.963	0.928	0.981	0.962
DI Combos * Fluency 2	0.656	0.430	0.901	0.812
RL Combos * Fluency 2	0.709	0.502	0.931	0.867

Participants who speak at a faster overall speed (articulation rate) in tasks accomplished more RL and DI combos in the experiment, which reflects that speed fluency can boost overall proficiency in terms of complexity, accuracy, and fluency. When participants were more proficient with the provided templates, they were able to perform a 40-second recording after identifying the type of image presented in a describe image task, or together with the aid of notes-taken when undertaking a retell lecture task.

Participants practice with a simple template until they can achieve 100% fluency. Most participants were fluency-error free after 7 online sessions with templates applied in the describe image and retell lecture experiment, practicing with an average of 100 images and participating in 60 sessions (self-regulated home sessions included). Better syntactic complexity, and semantic accuracy can be achieved with further practice and participants' unconscious modification to the templates, being more flexible in terms of applying sentence structures and in being able to use more advanced vocabulary when approaching describe image and retell lecture tasks. This is an approach relying on strategic and flexible planning and involving participant meta-cognition, with descriptive knowledge and operation over their own cognitive process assists in constituting a repertoire of meta-cognitive self-instructions for the regulation of cognitive describe image and retell lecture task performance.

Research Question Results

Research Question One

Are working memory strategies constructs effective for answering PTEA speaking items?

Working memory strategy use is embedded in all three experiments, and applied with participants during online sessions, and utilized in their continued self-regulated home practice. The efficacy of these working memory strategies is measured by comparing speaking scores from the participant PTEA reports, comparing pre- and post-treatment PTEA score reports. Score report data reliability for initial and second PTEA score reports hold a Cronbach's alpha of 0.824 (r = 0.701, significant at the 0.000 level). Results of a paired samples t-test (see table 9) show a raise in mean scores for speaking in the PTEA from that of 63.83 to 74.50 after treatment, fluency mean scores rise from 66.05 to 75.41, and vocabulary mean scores rise from 63.77 to 69.20. Overall, mean scores rise from 65.06 to 72.98, suggesting that the working memory strategies applied in treatment (across all three experiments) were effective in leading to increased levels of fluency for these participants, and to a gradual improvement in pronunciation and vocabulary (with a 95% confidence interval difference, with all measures significant at the 0.000 level, with vocabulary $0.001 < 0.005$). Of note also, a positive correlation was found between test-takers' initial overall score and their desired target score (r = 0.605, p = 0.000), with Cohen's d supporting an almost large effect size for treatment improving in Overall score (*Cohen's d* = 0.73), especially in speaking (*Cohen's d* = 0.75), fluency (*Cohen's d* = 0.51), and vocabulary (*Cohen's d* = 0.51). This potentially indicates that if students are only able to undertake one of the study strategies then they are best engaging with speaking activities over fluency and vocabulary ones, as engaging with all three shows a similar effect size.

Table 9.

Paired Samples T-Test Results

	PTEA Test Score	N	Std. Deviation	Std. Error Mean	Mean	Cohen's d
Pair 1	Overall 1	107	11.59	1.12	65.06	
	Overall 2	107	10.11	0.98	72.98	0.73
Pair 2	Speaking 1	107	17.13	1.66	63.83	
	Speaking 2	107	13.67	1.32	74.50	0.75
Pair 3	Fluency1	107	20.88	2.02	66.05	
	Fluency 2	107	15.48	1.50	75.41	0.51
Pair 4	Vocabulary 1	107	16.06	1.55	63.77	
	Vocabulary 2	107	14.56	1.41	69.20	0.35

Research Question Two

Are cognitive factors influential in explaining variances in speaking performance for those sitting the PTEA?

By encouraging participants to achieve combos across all three experiments, it was determined that participant cognitive factors in terms of controlling anxiety, their attention, their speed fluency, and response latency are influential factors in explaining variance in speaking performance on the PTEA test. Moreover, it was also determined that setting a target score before engaging in treatment sessions, served as a strong motivation for participants as it was a predictor of participant devotion to time on task during treatment sessions and during their self-regulated home practice. Through the three experiments it was also found that participants were able to generate meta-cognitive strategies that allowed them to self-regulate their complexity, accuracy and fluency in speaking. All of these findings provide implications regarding the importance of matching learners' meta-cognition with WM strategies in order to optimize instructional outcomes.

General Discussion, Limitations and Future Research Possibilities

Findings provide a basis for the pro-fluency strategy use in PTEA, due to its Computer Assisted Language Testing (CALT) nature. Human raters may be more adequate judging the accurate choice of vocabulary in a context, however, we noted for the PTEA, that fluency-oriented training suffices for most test-takers to meet their target score in a relative shorter period of time. In contrast, if learners spend a long time updating their vocabulary scale, improving their pronunciation, or trying to produce with situation-mediated accuracy and complexity when undertaking the actual test, anxiety in being logically organized and any lack of confidence will significantly affect their fluency, which would result in a less than satisfactory score in terms of their indicated desired PTEA score.

Cognitive factors that impact fluency are those that are task-based and strategy-mediated. How well/fast test-takers process specific stimuli can then help them decide about the nature of that stimuli, or the successful parsing of a sentence in stimulating fluency in recall in the read aloud experiment; the homogeneity of the cognitive processes when encoding and retrieving information can also largely determine fluency as shown in the repeat sentence – answer short question experiment; it was also found that flexibility in processing is prominent when distinguishing closed skills in predictable environments from open skills in variable and interactive circumstances. For example, the use of a visuospatial sketchpad, episodic buffer and note-taking skills can establish a predictable environment for test-takers. If test takers need to improve speaking scores in a short period of time, then production and comprehension needs to be mediated by instruction and mnemonic strategies. Templates for describe image and retell lecture tasks are effective in improving fluency by reducing initial-phase syntactic and lexical complexity, and possibly trading off accuracy.

However, under the washback hypothesis (Alderson & Wall, 1993) and the strategy-mediated hypothesis (Dunning & Holmes, 2014), strategies towards a possible tradeoff among complexity, accuracy, and fluency are too pragmatic in a computer-based test. This is because it takes a learned and better cognitive control for working memory training efficacy to transfer to other untrained tasks and only after a new cognitive skill has been acquired can working memory strategies be transferred to a new task for long-term enhancement in learning aptitude (Fellman et al, 2020). This provides grounds for our consideration of cognitive factors from the experiments to apply to daily L2 learning and training, and in the influence of strategy use, in the speed of processing, the capacity of working memory, and as predictors of good pronunciation in an artificial intelligence context (such as that of the computer based PTEA test).

Further, task-based memory tests indicate strategies such as the template treatment applied during the describe image and retell lecture experiment proving effective in improving fluency by reducing complexity and accuracy. Further studies would need a bigger sample base, to consider observable longitudinal effects of cognitive factors, such as the nature of attention and confidence from which working memory efficacy is impacted. Also, since PTEA is based on the scoring mechanism of current artificial intelligence (AI) maturity, the working memory training process and pertinence may deviate due to emphasis placed on passive output with a computer and algorithmic use of complexity, accuracy, and fluency elements, and as a result also of ignoring the primary communicative nature of languages. A problem we detected during the experiment is that female shrill voices are difficult for AI at this time, resulting in a minimum score of 10 out of 90 for both pronunciation and fluency based on the official reporting algorithm for participants with such a voice. The question that emerges here then is whether or not contemporary AI speech recognition technology is accurate enough for high-stakes computer-based tests like the PTEA, and whether increasing task authenticity will lead to fuzziness of test construct validity according to requirements for corpus and the necessity of more strategies in language assessment. This fuzziness creates the space and necessity for future research on PTEA strategies both linguistically and cognitively.

Conclusion

Linguistic complexity, accuracy, and fluency measures can present various underlying sub-constructs in different tasks, for example, components that explain variances for speaking performance in this study are lexical complexity, phonological accuracy and fluency which are reflected by participant articulation speed, speech breakdowns and speech repairs. Fluency is the most decisive component that explains the most variance in PTEA speaking performance, and strategies can be tailored for PTEA tasks to address this issue. To this end, the results of this paper indicate that the use of preliminary fluency-oriented strategies are able to improve speaking performance rapidly and lead to longitudinal lexical complexity and phonological accuracy transfer when cognitive factors related to working memory training are taken into consideration.

References

Akan, M., Stanley, S. E., & Benjamin, A. S. (2018). Testing enhances memory for context. *Journal of Memory and Language, 103*, 19–27.

Alderson, C., & Wall, D. (1993). Does washback exist? *Applied Linguistics, 14*(2), 115-129.

Baddeley, A. (2000). The episodic buffer: A new component of working memory? *Trends in Cognitive Sciences, 4*, 417–23.

Baddeley, A. D. (1986). *Working memory.* Clarendon Press.

Baese-Berk, M., & Samuel, A. (2016). Listeners beware: Speech production may be bad for learning speech sounds. *Journal of Memory and Language, 89*, 23–36.

Bailey, H., Dunlosky, J., & Kane, M. J. (2011). Contribution of strategy use to performance on complex and simple span tasks. *Memory and Cognition 39*(3), 46-87.

Bein, O., Trzewik, M., & Maril, A. (2019). The role of prior knowledge in incremental associative learning: An empirical and computational approach. *Journal of Memory and Language, 107*, 1–24.

Bosker, H., Pinget, A., Quene, H., Sanders, T., & de Jong, N. (2013). What makes speech sound fluent? The contributions of pauses, speed and repairs. *Language Testing, 30*, 159–175.

Burgess, N., & Hitch, G. J. (1999). Memory for serial order: A network model of the phonological loop and its timing. *Psychological Review, 106*(3), 551.

Camos, V., Lagner, P., & Barrouillet, P. (2009). Two maintenance mechanisms of verbal information in working memory. *Journal of Memory and Language, 61*(3), 457–469.

Clark, H. H., & Krych, M. A. (2004). Speaking while monitoring addressees for understanding. *Journal of Memory and Language, 50*(1), 62–81.

Cowan, N., Braine, M. D. S., & Leavitt, L. A. (1985). The phonological and meta-phonological representation of speech: Evidence from fluent backward talkers. *Journal of Memory and Language, 24*(6), 679–698.

Cox, J. G. (2017). Explicit instruction, bilingualism, and the older adult learner. *Studies in Second Language Acquisition, 39*(1), 29–58.

Culbertson, J., Gagliardi, A., & Smith, K. (2017). Competition between phonological and semantic cues in noun class learning. *Journal of Memory and Language, 92*, 343–358.

Dabrowska, E. (2008). The effects of frequency and neighborhood density on adult speakers' productivity with Polish case inflections: An empirical test of usage-based approaches to morphology. *Journal of Memory and Language, 58*(4), 931–951.

Daneman, M., & Carpenter, P. A. (1980). Individual differences in working memory and reading. *Journal of Verbal Learning & Verbal Behavior, 19*, 450–66.

De Jong, N. H., Steinel, M. P., Florijn, A. F., Schoonen, R., & Hulstijn, J. H. (2012). Facets of speaking proficiency. *Studies in Second Language Acquisition, 34*(1), 5–34.

Derwing, T. M., Rossiter, M. J., Munro, M. J., & Thomson, R. I. (2004). Second language fluency: Judgements on different tasks. *Language Learning, 54*, 655–679.

Psychonomic Bulletin & Review, 23(1), 306–316. Dunning, D. L., & Holmes, J. (2014). Does working memory training promote the use of strategies on untrained working memory tasks? *Memory and Cognition, 42*(6), 854–862.

Ellis, R., & Yuan, F. (2004). the Effects of Planning on Fluency, Complexity, and Accuracy in Second Language Narrative Writing. *Studies in Second Language Acquisition, 26*(1), 59–84.

Fellman, Jylkkä, Waris, Soveri, Ritakallio, Haga, Laine. (2020). The role of strategy use in working memory training outcomes. *Journal of Memory and Language, 110,* 104064.

Ferreira, F. (2000). Syntax in language production: An approach using tree-adjoining grammars. In L. Wheeldon (Ed.), *Aspects of language production* (pp.291–330). Psychology Press/Taylor & Francis.

Freed, E. M., Hamilton, S. T., & Long, D. L. (2017). Comprehension in proficient readers: The nature of individual variation. *Journal of Memory and Language, 97,* 135–153.

Gathercole, S. E., & Baddeley, A. D. (1990). Phonological memory deficits in language disordered children: Is there a causal connection? *Journal of Memory and Language, 29(3),* 336–360.

Gathercole, S. E., & Baddeley, A. D. (1993). *Working memory and language.* Psychology Press.

Gathercole, S. E., Dunning, D. L., Holmes, J., & Norris, D. (2019). Working memory training involves learning new skills. *Journal of Memory and Language, 105,* 19–42.

Gavens, N., & Barrouillet, P. (2004). Delays of retention, processing efficiency, and attentional resources in working memory span development. *Journal of Memory and Language, 51(4),* 644–657.

Granena, G. (2019). Cognitive aptitudes and L2 speaking proficiency. *Studies in Second Language Acquisition, 41(2),* 313–336.

Gray, S., Green, S., Alt, M., Hogan, T., Kuo, T., Brinkley, S., & Cowan, N. (2017). The structure of working memory in young children and its relation to intelligence. *Journal of Memory and Language, 92,* 183–201.

Grimshaw, J., & Cardoso, W. (2018). Activate space rats! Fluency development in a mobile game-assisted environment. *Language Learning and Technology, 22*(3), 159–175.

Gupta, P., & Tisdale, J. (2009). Does phonological short-term memory causally determine vocabulary learning? Toward a computational resolution of the debate. *Journal of Memory and Language, 61*(4), 481–502.

Higgs, T. V., & Clifford, R. (1982). The push toward communication. In T. V. Higgs (Ed.), *Curriculum, competence and the foreign language teacher* (pp. 243-265). National Textbook Company.

Housen, A., & Simoens, H. (2016). Introduction: Cognitive perspectives on difficulty and complexity in L2 acquisition. *Studies in Second Language Acquisition, 38*(2), 163-175.

Housen, A., Kuiken, F., & Vedder, I. (2012). *Dimensions of L2 performance and proficiency: Complexity, accuracy and fluency in SLA.* John Benjamins Publishing Company.

Hsu, H. C. (2017). The effect of task planning on L2 performance and L2 development in text-based synchronous computer-mediated communication. *Applied Linguistics, 38*(3), 359–385.

Hughes, R. W., Chamberland, C., Tremblay, S., & Jones, D. M. (2016). Perceptual-motor determinants of auditory-verbal serial short-term memory. *Journal of Memory and Language, 90*, 126–146.

Lambert, C., & Kormos, J. (2014). Complexity, accuracy, and fluency in task-based l2 research: toward more developmentally based measures of second language acquisition. *Applied Linguistics, 35*(5), 607–614.

Lee, J. S., & Lee, K. (2019). Affective factors, virtual intercultural experiences, and L2 willingness to communicate in in-class, out-of-class, and digital settings. *Language Teaching Research, 21*(3), 167-182.

Levelt, W. J. M. (1989). *Speaking.* MIT Press.

Lilienthal, L., Tamez, E., Shelton, J. T., Myerson, J., & Hale, S. (2013). Dual n-back training increases the capacity of the focus of attention. *Psychonomic Bulletin & Review, 20*(1), 135–141.

McManus, K., & Marsden, E. (2017). L1 explicit instruction can improve L2 online and offline performance. *Studies in Second Language Acquisition, 39*(3), 459–492.

McNamara, D. S., & Scott, J. L. (2001). Working memory capacity and strategy use. *Memory & Cognition, 29*(1), 10–17.

Messick, S. (1992). Validity of test interpretation and use. In M.C. Alkin (ed.), *Encyclopedia of Educational Research* (6th ed.). Macmillan.

Mulligan, N. W., Susser, J. A., & Smith, S. A. (2016). The testing effect is moderated by experimental design. *Journal of Memory and Language, 90*, 49–65.

Munezane, Y. (2015). Enhancing willingness to communicate: Relative effects of visualization and goal setting. *Modern Language Journal, 99*(1), 175–191.

Onaha, H. (2004). Effect of shadowing and dictation on listening comprehension ability of Japanese EFL learners based on the theory of working memory. *JACET Bulletin, 39*, 137–48.

Öztekin, I., & McElree, B. (2007). Proactive interference slows recognition by eliminating fast assessments of familiarity. *Journal of Memory and Language, 57*(1), 126–149.

Pallotti, G. (2009). CAF: Defining, refining and differentiating constructs. *Applied Linguistics, 30*, 590–610.

Pan, S. C., Pashler, H., Potter, Z. E., & Rickard, T. C. (2015). Testing enhances learning across a range of episodic memory abilities. *Journal of Memory and Language, 83*, 53–61. https://doi.org/10.1016/j.jml.2015.04.001

Pearson. (2010). *The official guide to Pearson test of English academic.* Longman.

Pearson. (2011). *PTE academic tutorial.* Longman.

Pearson. (2012). *Score guide*. Longman

Peng, P., & Fuchs, D. (2017). A randomized control trial of working memory training with and without strategy instruction: Effects on young children's working memory and comprehension. *Journal of Learning Disabilities, 50*(1), 62–80.

Ren, W. (2014). A longitudinal investigation into L2 learners' cognitive processes during study abroad. *Applied Linguistics, 35*(5), 575–594.

Robey, A. (2019). The benefits of testing: Individual differences based on student factors. *Journal of Memory and Language, 108,* 104029.

Robinson, P.(2003). 'Attention and memory during SLA' in C. J. Doughty and M. H. Long (eds): *The Handbook of Second Language Acquisition*. Blackwell Publishing.

Robinson, P. (2002). Individual differences in intelligence, aptitude and working memory during adult incidental second language learning: A replication and extension of Reber, Walkenfeld, and Hernstadt (1991). In P. Robinson (Ed.), *Individual differences and instructed language learning* (pp. 211–266). John Benjamins Publishing Company.

Sakai, H. (2018). Working Memory in Listening. *The TESOL Encyclopedia of English Language Teaching* (pp. 1-6). John Wiley & Sons.

Samuel, A. G., & Larraza, S. (2015). Does listening to non-native speech impair speech perception? *Journal of Memory and Language, 81,* 51–71.

Skehan, P. (2009). Modelling second language performance: integrating complexity, accuracy, fluency, lexis. *Applied Linguistics, 30*(4), 1–23.

Suzuki, S., & Kormos, J. (2019). Linguistic dimensions of comprehensibility and perceived fluency: an investigation of complexity, accuracy and fluency in second language argumentative speech. *Studies in Second Language Acquisition, 42*(1), 1–25.

Tavakoli, P., & Skehan, P. (2005). Strategic planning, task structure, and performance testing. In R. Ellis (Ed.), *Planning and task performance in a second language* (pp. 239–273). John Benjamins Publishing Company.

Van Batenburg, E. S. L., Oostdam, R. J., Van Gelderen, A. J. S., Fukkink, R. G., & De Jong, N. H. (2019). Oral interaction in the EFL classroom: The effects of instructional focus and task type on learner affect. *Modern Language Journal, 103*(1), 308–326.

Vercellotti, M. (2017). The development of complexity, accuracy, and fluency in second language performance: A longitudinal study. *Applied Linguistics, 38*(1), 90–111.

Wei, W., & Zheng, Y. (2017). An investigation of integrative and independent listening test tasks in a computerized academic English test. *Computer Assisted Language Learning, 30*(8), 864–883.

Xie, Z., & Dong, Y. (2017). Contributions of bilingualism and public speaking training to cognitive control differences among young adults. *Bilingualism, 20*(1), 55–68.

Zahedi, K. & Shamsaee, S. (2012). Viability of construct validity of the speaking modules of international language examinations (IELTS vs. TOEFL iBT): Evidence from Iranian test takers. *Educational Assessment, Evaluation and Accountability, 24*(3), 263-277.

Zheng, Y., & De Jong, J. (2011). Research Notes: *Establishing construct and concurrent validity of Pearson Test of English Academic*. Pearson Education Ltd.

3. Time-Saving Dynamic Rubrics for Effective Online Feedback and Scoring

Jan Mathys de Beer
Woosong University

Abstract

There are many advantages to online language teaching, but one of the great disadvantages is not being able to easily provide personalized feedback to students so they can improve in the areas where they are struggling. This becomes a particularly difficult task with large class sizes or when scheduled with many classes to teach. Yet, electronic dynamic rubrics can prove to be time-saving and effective for providing both constructive feedback and in providing ways to connect your feedback to the marks of a student. Getting the balance right between coaching students' language learning and showing them how they have improved is not an easy task. This chapter provides the reader with practical examples to develop their own time-saving, effective dynamic rubrics for online, hybrid, and traditional classroom contexts.

Introduction

It is the year 2021 and as I am writing this chapter, the spring semester is upon us. At my educational institution, lecturers and students alike suddenly had to adjust to a new mode of online teaching and learning with the start of the previous spring semester, exactly one year ago, as a result of the notorious Coronavirus. We don't know what the future might hold, but one thing is for sure, some form of online teaching will remain part of our world for at least another year or so, if not for good. Will we ever return to face-to-face classes as before 2020, or indeed in the way they were delivered then? This remains to be seen. There is a suspicion that we will probably retain at least some form of hybrid online-offline teaching methodology in times to come. We are also aware of the big downside that the online teaching environment can provide, widening the equity gap between developed and developing countries where the students from low-income and other marginalized groups seem to have suffered the most from the pandemic (Atherton, 2020), and what is addressed in this chapter is not insensitive to this reality.

An interesting survey (Miyagawa & Perdue, 2020) on the practice of teaching during the pandemic found that for some teachers and students, the move to online teaching has been traumatic, while for others it has been a welcome improvement. Especially those with labs, and those who focus on hands-on training, found the online environment difficult. But some instructors were excited about the opportunities that came with teaching online, such as incorporating guest lecturers from around the world, or collaborating with lecturers teaching similar courses at other institutions. The surprising element in this survey was that many lecturers grappled with assessments. The issues mentioned are those relating to the difficulty of designing tests that students could not cheat on and the best ways to proctor such tests. This raises the question, understandably, why are we (still) testing students in this way? One response was that it's because we have been doing it the same way for 50 years. Some institutions decided to relax their requirements for assessment, and some lecturers reduced the number of quizzes and eliminated some exams. What we learn from this is that online teaching greatly changes the nature of assessment and the ways in which we can provide feedback to our students.

In my own transition from the traditional face-to-face teaching setting to an online teaching context using Zoom in 2020, assessment and giving feedback were important factors to reconsider. During 2020, I was teaching English writing courses, which have their own assessment challenges. Firstly, I had to check students' work as they progressed with a writing assignment, and, secondly, I had to provide individualized feedback to ensure that they recognized the mistakes or errors that they had made, in order to learn from then and so as not to repeat them. Thirdly, I had to provide a final score and feedback based on a rubric at the completion of assessment and do so by a fixed date. The same scoring rubric was to be used for the two institutionally required exams, a midterm and final. Feedback was very important for the midterm exam in order to prevent students from making the same mistakes or errors later on in the final exam. So, I had to go back to the drawing board and ensure that my teaching goals were aligned with my rubric and then I had to ensure that the marks reflected not only the level on which the students wrote, but also the level of their understanding of the main aims of the course and the expectations that were outlined for them. This exercise proved to be time-consuming at first, but once the goals and points of the rubric were aligned, the assessment became time-saving and quite effective.

This chapter discusses the process of developing a valid and reliable rubric for assessing language skills for use in an online class setting. It will start with looking at some basic requirements for skills assessment and then move on to an example of redesigning an ordinary writing rubric into a dynamic rubric using a Microsoft Excel* spreadsheet. It will then discuss the application and use of such a dynamic rubric and conclude with ideas to use dynamic rubrics in different classroom settings. By

---

* For this chapter, use is made of Microsoft Excel 2016. Note that there might be slight variations if using earlier or later versions of the software. However, the basic principles and processes should remain similar across all versions of the product.

the end of this chapter, the reader will have practical examples that should assist them to develop their own time-saving, effective dynamic rubrics for use from within online, hybrid, and traditional classroom contexts.

Some Considerations for Valid and Reliable Assessment-Feedback

Two important qualities that assessment should display are *validity* and *reliability* (Chapelle & Brindley, 2002). The most basic form of validity is displayed in a test with specific questions and answers, based on the content of a course, for example, detailed questions about times and dates of events in a history lesson. If the answers to the questions are not found in the content of the course, the validity of the test is questionable. In language learning, a valid assessment should test the *skill* we have in mind and nothing else. In this case, the assessment should allow the student to produce the skills that were taught in the course. If you want to test whether a person can read in English and understand what they are reading, you would not ask the person to write a paragraph. In order to create a valid test, the person has to read set material and then you would ask questions to test their understanding of what they have just read. The questions should either be based on information given in the set reading or on implied information available to the reader from the text, with the assessor asking nothing outside the scope of the reading provided. An assessment of language writing should be in agreement with the level of the students as well as with the learning outcomes of the course. For example, if the perfect tense was not part of the course outcomes, students should not be penalized for the incorrect usage of this tense, but they may be penalized for using the perfect tense instead of the tense required in the course or the particular assessment item. So, the validity of a language skills rubric is increased by developing the different items of the rubric in connection with the skills taught during the course on the level of the students in question.

For assessment to be reliable, it should be designed in such a way that different assessors in different contexts would yield the same result when using that particular instrument of assessment. An answer key with specific answers on specific questions is significantly more reliable than a rubric that assesses speaking fluency, because specific answers are much more defined than the level of a student's ability in an oral exam. For this reason, designing a reliable rubric for writing or speaking assessment is more complex than compiling an answer key for multiple choice questions. Rubrics are used for assessing speaking and writing ability in language learning when students are producing written or oral work that may take on indefinite possible forms. Thus, in order to develop a reliable and valid writing or speaking assessment rubric, it is important to keep the level of the students and the specific learning outcomes of the course in mind.

Rubrics are often provided for teachers and lecturers in language learning programs by their schools, institutions, or supervisors. However, it remains the responsibility of the teacher to ensure that their assessment is valid and reliable. This is especially important in the context of online teaching, since students in an online classroom rely heavily on the feedback that they receive in the form of a scoring rubric in order to determine whether or not they are performing at the required level, and if not, where they should begin to focus in order to improve. The advantage of providing individualized feedback to students through a well-designed scoring rubric is that the assessment, grading, and student feedback happens simultaneously, saving the lecturer considerable time in contrast to doing assessment for grading purposes and providing feedback as two separate actions. It is also beneficial to the students because, by looking at their feedback/scoring rubric, they can then see both where they lost points and what errors contributed to that loss. The educational value of this simultaneous scoring and error-identifying process is that students learn through the feedback provided how they can improve on their errors. In my experience, online students in particular appreciated this kind of feedback since it is direct, understandable, and can lead them to improve. These factors of reliability, validity, and assessment-feedback should be kept in mind when a standard rubric is converted into a dynamic rubric. These introductory remarks should suffice as a caution when you redesign any rubric into a dynamic one, taking care not to make any changes that affect the validity and reliability that has been built into the original.

Redesigning a Rubric into a Dynamic Rubric

It is not the focus of this chapter to provide a reliable and validated rubric for any English language skill. That would be a topic on its own and there is a wealth of literature on this subject (see for example Coombe et al., 2012; specifically Davidson & Fulcher, 2012; Ioannou-Georgiou, 2003). The example presented is fictional for the purpose of illustration and should not be used for language assessment. This is deliberate, avoiding the provision of a complete rubric as an example, as the purpose of the chapter is to focus on the process of converting a standard rubric into a dynamic rubric so that the reader can then apply this process to any rubric that their needs might require throughout the course of their career.

There are basically two types of rubrics that can be used for language testing: holistic and analytical (Konrad et al., 2018). Both types can be adjusted into a dynamic form, however, the holistic rubric will function much simpler than the analytical one. The holistic type rubric is designed to assess different aspects of language (e.g., task achievement, range of grammar and vocabulary, organization and cohesion, accuracy of grammar, vocabulary, and spelling) with a single score on the basis of overall impression (Hughes, 1989), and it works more like a scale than a checklist. In this kind of rubric, a student cannot score high on 'task achievement' and low on 'range of grammar and vocabulary'. The different aspects that are assessed (e.g., task achievement) will all be judged on one holistic level. The scale of an holistic rubric can still be used as a dynamic rubric, but the teacher will only be able to select one level as the score, which means that individualized feedback should be given in, for example, a comment box. An analytical rubric may have more detailed items that are graded, and this kind of rubric is more suitable for providing individualized feedback because each category of language can be assessed individually for each student. This means that less additional information is needed in a comment section. This is the kind of rubric that is used as exemplar in this chapter.

In the following example, we will describe how an ordinary analytical writing rubric can be redesigned and converted into a dynamic one for use in a Microsoft Excel environment. The first step is to format the rubric into a table and separate each descriptor into its own cell, with headings on one axis and scores on the other (see figure 1). In this example, the score is at the top and the subject headings are on the left-hand side, but they can also be transposed. However, for a dynamic rubric it is advisable to place the scores at the top so that each heading can be easily scored on the right-hand side. The points may also sequence from low to high or high to low, depending on the teacher's preference. This table should then be imported or copy-pasted into a new Microsoft Excel spreadsheet.

The next step is to design a way to select and highlight different cells (i.e., different descriptions) in the copy-pasted table. A simple way to do this is to make sure that the descriptions in each cell do not contain any full-stops or periods.

Then, the teacher can simply select the relevant cell description by adding a period at the end of the descriptor in that cell (see cells D2, B3, C4, E5, F6 in Figure 1). For example, if we want to choose the descriptor for cell C2, 'Ideas relevant to the task' in the first category (Ideas), we will simply add a period (.) at the end of the phrase: 'Ideas relevant to the task'. This period will be the marker on which the score will be calculated and on which the format (highlighting) of the cell will be based.

Figure 1.

Example Dynamic Rubric

	A	B	C	D	E	F	G
1	Category	4	3	2	1	0	Score
2	Ideas	Wide range of ideas relevant to the task	Ideas relevant to task	Generally addresses the task.	Attempts the task with few ideas	Ideas and content not relevant to the task	2
3	Content development	Content points fully developed.	Development of content points	Some development of content	Lacking development of content	Confusing information and ideas, with no attempt at cohesion	4
4	Cohesion	Manages all aspects of cohesion well	Uses a range of cohesive devices appropriately.	Some attempts at cohesive devices	Rare or incorrect use of cohesive devices	Evidence of lengthy text translated directly	3
5	Vocabulary	Wide range of vocabulary	Good range of vocabulary	Reasonable range of structures	Limited range of vocabulary used.	Inadequate vocabulary or plagiarism	1
6	Artwork & referencing	Artwork & referencing perfect	Artwork & referencing good	Artwork & referencing average	Inappropriate art & referencing	Artwork lacking.	0

Calculating the scores for each row

The mathematical part of creating a dynamic rubric, is calculating the scores and highlighting the relevant cells. If you are a novice with Microsoft Excel, the following may sound technical, but it is a simple process that you should be able to follow and work out after short trial and error. If you are anything more than a beginner, it should be no problem for you.

First, the scores of the selected cells (selected by adding a period at the end of the description as previously explained) should be calculated. In the example here, we will use column G for the score calculation, while row 1 contains the score values. This will be done with a formula that looks at the rightmost character of each cell in the row, and if that character is a period (.), the score of that column in row 1 of that cell will be used. The basic formula for looking at the rightmost character of cell B2 is:

```
=IF(RIGHT(B2)=".",[value if true],[value if false])
```

However, we want to check the value of five cells (in columns B-F) and, if any of them has a period at the end of the cell, it should yield the value of that column in row 1. So, we will combine four 'IF' functions to check for a period in columns B through E, and if none of these are selected, the value should be zero, which is also the value of cells in that of column F. The combined formula for cell G2 would then look like this:

```
=IF(RIGHT(B2)=".",4,IF(RIGHT(C2)=".",3,IF(RIGHT(D2)=".",2,IF(RIGHT(E2)=".",1,0))))
```

The formula can be further automated by replacing the 'values if true' within the cells in row 1, as follows:

```
=IF(RIGHT(B2)=".",B$1,IF(RIGHT(C2)=".",C$1,IF(RIGHT(D2)=".",D$1,IF(RIGHT(E2)=".",E$1,0))))
```

If the value of column F was not zero, but, for example, 1, and the values of the other columns were adjusted accordingly (B-E = 5, 4, 3, 2) then one more basic formula will be added to the combined formula:

```
=IF(RIGHT(B2)=".",B$1,IF(RIGHT(C2)=".",C$1,IF(RIGHT(D2)=".",D$1,IF(RIGHT(E2)=".",E$1, (RIGHT(F2)=".",F$1,0)))))
```

The formula for the next row (G3) will then be adjusted accordingly:

```
=IF(RIGHT(B3)=".",B$1,IF(RIGHT(C3)=".",C$1,IF(RIGHT(D3)=".",D$1,IF(RIGHT(E3)=".",E$1, (RIGHT(F3)=".",F$1,0)))))
```

The dollar sign ($) before the number 1, referring to the value in row 1 (e.g., 'B$1') ensures that the 'value if true' always checks the relevant value in the score row. When the formula in G2 is copied to G3, G4, G5, and G6, the program should automatically adjust the formula for the rows, so the formulas for these cells do not need to be adjusted manually. You can test the formula by typing a period at the end of one of the cells and see if the correct number is displayed in the corresponding cell in column G. If the correct number does not display, then you will need to check that the formula is correct. Once the formula is working correctly, the next step is to highlight the cells marked with a period so that students will see which item applies to them.

Automatically highlighting cells

As part of their feedback, students should be able to see which cells in a dynamic rubric apply to their scoring. A good way to do this is to apply 'conditional formatting' to the cells of the rubric that need highlighting, and these would be one of those that have been formatted with a period at the end of the description in that cell. Conditional formatting should only be applied to the cells in the rubric that are used for scoring because it is based on the occurrence of a period in the relevant cell. If other cells contain periods, they will be wrongly formatted so it is important to take care to which cells you place a period.

In order to apply conditional formatting to the exemplar rubric, select all the cells that are used for scoring. In our example, this is cells B2 through to F6. Once these cells are selected, under the 'Home' tab (in Microsoft Excel), select the button 'Conditional formatting' by clicking on the down arrow. Then select the option 'Highlight Cells Rules' and select 'Text that contains…' to open a dialogue box (see figure 2). You can then specify what the program should look for in a cell in order to apply special formatting to that cell. In this example, the program must look for a period. So, in the open box under the line 'Format cells that contain the text:', fill in ['.'], and choose a format method in the dropdown menu on the right-hand side. You can choose one of the options (e.g., 'Light Red Fill with Dark Red Text'), or you can customize the format the way you wish the cell to be highlighted for students.

Figure 2.

Conditional Cell Formatting

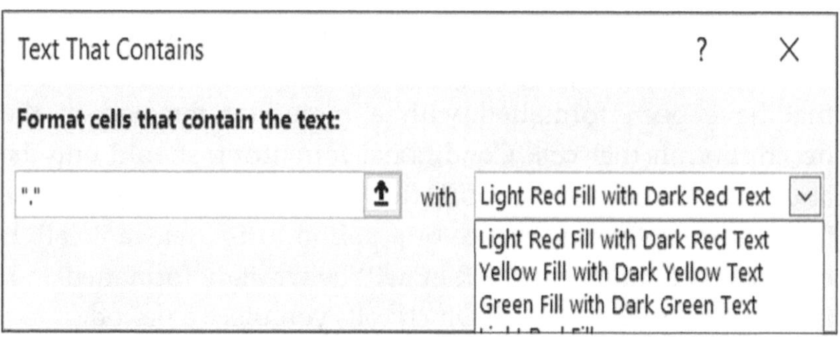

Following these steps will set up your cells (those with a period on the end of the text within them) so that the particular cell that needs highlighting for an individual student can be highlighted appropriately, either by shading or a color, so that they can see which aspect of the rubric reflects their work.

Automatically Calculate the Final Grade

For the more seasoned Microsoft Excel users, this paragraph is probably redundant, but for the sake of completeness, one should remember to set up the dynamic rubric so that the final grade is calculated automatically. In the exemplar used above (see figure 1), column G contains the scores for the individual sections of the rubric. However, in figure 3, the cell to the right of 'TOTAL POINT' contains the final score value (17), and to the right of this is the highest possible score (/20). In the cell that contains the final score value, the sum total of all the values in column G should be displayed. A simple =SUM(range of values) formula can provide this information, with 'range of values' containing the range of cells that contains the scores for the individual sections (see column G in figure 1). To calculate the final grade, as shown in the example provided in figure 1, assuming that figure 1 contains all the grading values, the following formula would apply:

```
=SUM(G2:G6)
```

Adding an 'Instructor Comments' Box

Depending on the detail of feedback that your rubric reflects in the different descriptors, it may be advisable to add an 'Instructor Comments' box to your rubric. This is especially important when you are using a holistic type rubric. I have found that instructor comments are more visible to students at the top of the rubric than when they are placed at the bottom, since students usually first look for their score, then look at any highlighted area on the rubric, and then sometimes disregard anything else below that. An instructor comments area can be added by merging a group of cells and providing them with a heading 'Instructor Comments', 'Teacher Feedback', or whatever you might prefer. Figure 3 provides a final exam rubric example with a 'Lecturer Comments Important! Please read' box located between the rubric and student details.

Any additional feedback that a student needs in order to improve can be provided in the instructor comment box. This is also a good place to write words of encouragement or to address specific mistakes or errors that a student has made in their work. This feedback also ensures that your rubric provides personalized information – something that is important in online and distance learning.

Figure 3.

Lecturer Comments Box

Final Exam Rubric					
			TOTAL POINT		**17** **/20**
STUDENT Number:		1234567	STUDENT Name:		Jane Doe
Lecturer Comments Important! Please read.		Good work! Remember to only make use of your notes when you write your paragraph. Check the spelling of "vegetables". Sentence 3: Only use a comma before "because" when you want to clarify the meaning of the sentence.			
Score Gradient	Notes and Planning	Content	Organization & Cohesion	Grammar & Vocab Range and Accuracy	Score
5	Plan and relevant notes demonstrated; The final writing clearly reflects the student's planning and notes	Wide range of ideas relevant to the task; all ideas developed fully and effectively	Valid ideas organized very effectively.	Wide range of vocab and structures used accurately and appropriately to express valid ideas	5

Duplicating the Master Rubric for Each Student

After the rubric has been provided with a heading (e.g., 'Assignment 1 Rubric' or 'Final Exam Rubric'), cells for student information (student number and name), and a cell for the final score/mark next to the highest score possible can be added (see figure 3), it should then be checked for errors. Save only the sheet (not the whole workbook) as a portable document file or PDF to see if it fits on the page the way you prefer, because this will be the document that each student will receive as feedback. You may then email the document to learners or upload it to the learner management system (LMS) for them to view/download from there. When you save a sheet as a PDF, you can either select all relevant cells and choose to save 'Selection' under 'Options' (in the 'Save As' dialogue box), or you can ignore the 'Options' button, in which case the program will save the active sheet by default, which is the fastest option. If the save sheet as a PDF does not produce the feedback document that you have in mind, make changes and save it again until you are happy with the final result. It is important to refine the master rubric in this way before you duplicate it for each student, because if there are any errors on the master and you duplicate it for every student in every single class that you teach, you will either have to correct each sheet for each student, or you will have to delete all of the sheets with errors, fix the master sheet, and then go through the PDF creation process again. The whole idea is that the rubric should be time-saving, and so checking each step is important as you progress through the conversion from a standard rubric to a dynamic one.

When you are satisfied with your master rubric sheet, rename the sheet to 'Master' and save a duplicate copy of the Microsoft Excel file so that you can retain an unaltered backup of your rubric. You can now go ahead and duplicate the 'Master' rubric sheet for each student. Rename each sheet with the name or student number of each individual student. For the more technically advanced readers, keep in mind that there are also ways to insert the name of the sheet into a cell in the rubric, so you only need to give each sheet the appropriate name and it will also be reflected on the rubric for each student. Here is the formula to insert the name of a sheet into a cell in that sheet:

```
=MID(CELL("filename",A1),FIND("]",CELL("filename",A1))+1,255)
```

Should you be using the same rubric for more than one assessment for your class, you can also duplicate the Microsoft Excel file with the already duplicated rubric sheets for each student and rename it to reflect the different assessment events for the course (e.g., 'Midterm Exam', 'Final Exam', 'Assignment 4').

Using the Dynamic Rubric for Grading and Feedback

After you have created your dynamic rubric, tested it, checked it, duplicated it for each student, and duplicated the set of sheets for each assessment event, you should be ready to use it for your assessments. After the students have submitted their work, ensure that you open the correct workbook for the concerned assessment and make sure that you are on the correctly named sheet for the student whose work you are scoring. All you need to do now is to select the relevant cells according to the student's work by adding a period at the end of the cell description, add feedback in the comments box, check that the final score has been calculated correctly and that the student's information on the sheet is correct. Then save the sheet in a dedicated folder for this assessment under the student's name or student number. It will save time if the sheet name and the feedback PDF both have the same name because you can then double click on the sheet name, copy it, go to 'Save As', and paste the sheet name in the 'File name' box, select 'PDF (*.pdf)' in the 'Save as type' dropdown menu, and click on the 'Save' button. Then, move on to the next student's work. In this way, it takes minutes to score each student's work accurately and in a way that contains enough feedback for the student to know how they can improve.

After you have scored all the students' work and saved each individual rubric as a feedback rubric, you can then send the PDF to each student to view their results. If you need to archive your assessments, simply print out all the PDF files.

Conclusion

A practical description of the process of developing a valid and reliable dynamic rubric for assessing language skills for use in an online class setting was provided by this chapter. Prior to this, a brief reminder of validity and reliability as two basic requirements for skills assessment to keep in mind throughout the process was introduced. After which, a hands-on example of converting a standard rubric into a dynamic rubric using Microsoft Excel was detailed. The application and use of such a dynamic rubric can save time while also providing a means for easily giving effective personalized feedback to learners, and it is one that can be used across the gamut of online, hybrid, and face-to-face classroom settings. It is hoped that the reader has gained practical guidance that they can now use to develop their own time-saving, effective dynamic rubrics for use with their learners, and in their teaching contexts, throughout their career.

References

Atherton, G. (2020, November 14). A moment to address digital poverty and embed HE equity. *University World News.* https://www.universityworldnews.com/post.php?story=2020 1113085637660

Chapelle, C. A., & Brindley, G. (2002). Assessment. In N. Schmitt (Ed.), *An Introduction to Applied Linguistics* (pp. 267-288). Oxford University Press.

Coombe, C., O'Sullivan, B., Davison, P., & Stoynoff, S. (Eds.). (2012). *The Cambridge guide to language assessment.* Cambridge University Press.

Fulcher, G. (2010). *Practical language testing,* (1st ed.). Routledge.

Davidson, F. and Fulcher, G. (2012). Test specifications. In C. Coombe, B. O'Sullivan, P. Davison, & S. Stoynoff (Eds.). *The Cambridge guide to language assessment* (pp. 59-65). Cambridge University Press.

Hughes, A. (1989). *Testing for language teachers.* Cambridge University Press.

Ioannou-Georgiou, S. (2003) *Assessing young learners.* Oxford University Press.

Konrad, E., Holzknecht, F., Schwarz, V., & Spottl, C. (2018). *Assessing writing at lower levels: research findings, task development locally and internationally, and the opportunities presented by the extended CEFR descriptors* (Technical Report: AR-G/2018/4). British Council. https://doi.org/10.13140/RG.2.2.34667.80165

Miyagawa, S., & Perdue, M. (2020, November 11). A renewed focus on the practice of teaching. *Inside Higher Ed.* https://www.insidehighered.com/advice/2020/11/11/switching-online-teaching-during-pandemic-may-fundamentally-change-how-faculty

4. Integrated Approaches Using Student Generated Content

Andrew Aguiar
Gyeongsang National University

Nicole Shiosaki
Gyeongsang National University

Abstract

The pandemic emerging in 2020 has expanded online teaching methods through technological integration. One teaching approach that has benefited from online class provision is the use of student generated content. Student generated content allows language learners to interact with content made by other language learners. As all students require a device with internet access when teaching online, interacting with student generated content is much easier than in face-to-face contexts because students can conveniently interact through applications, such as Flipgrid. This gives students a chance to hear non-standard English, gives students ownership over their language learning and gives students a chance to interact with their peers in different ways. In order to gain the most from student generated content, the students' original outputs can be used as input for other students who utilize it to develop the next output in a student generated integrated skills approach. This presentation illustrates specific examples of activities and projects centered around using Flipgrid to create student generated content for learners to interact with while integrating multiple language skills into their development of student generated content. Post-pandemic, the methods used to develop an online student generated integrated approach can be worthwhile implementing from within the face-to-face classroom.

Introduction

The COVID-19 pandemic has forced educators to adapt to online teaching. With teaching online comes many problems that may or may not have been issues in for these educators in their physical classrooms. One of the main concerns, especially in the language teaching context, is enabling students to interact with each other when every student is in a different physical space. It is important for educators to address this issue as it can assist in ensuring the best possible learning environment for their students. Therefore, educators must adapt or create new approaches suitable for online teaching by taking advantage of online resources to enhance student interactivity.

One approach that has been successful while teaching university students taking a required online EFL course at a national university in South Korea is using student generated content (SGC) with an integrated language approach. Student generated content is a form of user-generated content. User-generated content being materials made by the users themselves rather than the primary producer. For example, making modifications to a game or making memes could be considered user-generated content, as these things are beyond the intention of the primary producer. Student generated content could be seen as the educational equivalent of user-generated content. Students create their own learning experience from existing materials as opposed to the teacher creating it for them (although the teacher may provide the materials from which to create the experience).

In conjunction with Nation's (2007) four strands and a little bit of technology, students are able to create their own content and interact with their peers' content in a shared online space. With some scaffolding and reliance on only a handful of applications, Flipgrid for creating videos, a word processor (e.g., Google Docs), and a learner management system (LMS; for example, Google Classroom), it is possible to employ a variety of SGC activities and projects, such as those described in this chapter, that put students at the center of their learning experience.

Literature Review

Student generated content

SGC is not a new concept. It has been used in science, teachnology, engineering, and math (STEM) classes (Arguello & Dempski, 2020; Bates et al., 2014; Luxton-Reilly et al., 2012; Pirhonen & Rasi, 2017), education (Wheeler et al., 2008; Yang et al., 2016), health education (Coulson & Frawley, 2017), and language teaching (Ktoridou & Doukanari, 2015; Shiosaki, 2020). SGC has also taken many forms within the classroom. It has been used to create comic books (Morrison et al., 2002), exam questions and answers (Bates et al., 2014; Lee, 2020; Luxton-Reilley et al., 2012), peer assessment (Arruabarrena et al., 2019), video projects (Arruabarrena et al., 2019; Coulson & Frawley, 2017; Pirhonen & Rasi, 2017) and wikis and blogs (Lee & McLoughlin, 2007; Ktoridou & Doukanari, 2015; Wheeler et al., 2008; Yang et al., 2016). Furthermore, with the ever-expanding online world, the potential combinations of online resources with SGC are only limited by the number and variety of tools available for learners to innovate with technology.

Benefits of SGC

Several common benefits have arisen in the literature regarding SGC implementation. First, students generally react positively to SGC approaches (Arguello & Dempski, 2020; Persada et al., 2020; Pirhonen & Rasi, 2017). It also increased online interactivity between students (Ktoridou & Doukanari, 2015; Yang et al., 2016). Secondly, development of student generated content led to higher levels of thinking as students had to deeply understand the content and draw from other knowledge areas to complete their tasks (Arruabarrena et al., 2019; Bates et al., 2014; Yang et al.,

2016). For example, when students were asked to create their own exam questions, the questions were usually more in depth than those created for students by educators (Bates et al., 2014). Furthermore, students were self-critical and held themselves to higher expectations (Luxton-Reilly et al., 2012). Development of SGC also leads to self-assessment as learners judge their own work and redo sections according to their own satisfaction/standards (Dyson, 2012; Luxton-Reilly et al., 2012). Third, students were motivated by making SGC (Dyson, 2012; Pirhonen & Rasi, 2017;). Persada et al. (2020) found access to technology and the internet to develop SGC content gave students options to control the type of content being developed and increased their motivation as a result. Furthermore, students were also motivated by knowing that their work was more than just a product to be graded, but a resource that would be useful in the future (Arruabarrena et al., 2019; Pirhonen & Rasi, 2017).

Workload can be reduced from utilizing SGC. Instead of the educator creating content or resources for their classes, the content made by students can be used as materials for future iterations of a class. For example, students can make instructional videos (Arruabarrena et al., 2019) or their own 3D models of chemical structures (Arguello & Dempski, 2020). Similarly, peer feedback can help reduce the amount of time educators spend giving feedback (Lee, 2020; Luxton-Reilley et al., 2012; Yang et al., 2016). However, SGC also brings concerns about increased workload. The amount of communication between students could make it difficult for teachers to check for content errors (Arruabarrena et al., 2019). However, this may be alleviated if there is a check at the end of the process (Lee, 2020). For example, a peer assessment approach can have students rate the correctness of content and student consensus will find the most correct answers (Luxton-Reilley et al., 2012).

Concerns with SGC

When it comes to utilizing SGC, there are several things to keep in mind. First, scaffolding enhances the process (Arruabarrena et al., 2019; Bates et al., 2014; Coulson & Frawley, 2017; Dyson, 2012; Wheeler et al., 2008). Students may have trouble using new technology despite perhaps being considered so-called digital natives, so they may require additional guidance (Wheeler et al., 2008). Online privacy is another consideration when students do work relying on open online resources, like wikis, as anyone is able to access their materials (Dyson, 2012; McLoughlin & Lee, 2010; Wheeler et al., 2008). Thus, having websites and other online resources that potentially ensure a safe harbor for learners is important when incorporating SGCs online.

Integrated skills approach

In the integrated skills approach, multiple skills, primarily listening, speaking, reading, and writing, are "interwoven in positive ways" to lead to language learning (Oxford, 2001, p. 2). Some skills are intuitively paired, such as speaking with pronunciation (Levis & Grant, 2003), speaking with listening and reading with writing (Pysarchyk & Yamshynska, 2015). The integrated skills approach also assumes that effort spent learning strategies in one area is also beneficial to all other areas. So, language learning strategies can be applied across all language skills (Kebede, 2013; Mekheimer, 2011; Oxford, 2001; Pysarchyk & Yamshynska, 2015).

The integrated skills approach has many advantages for language learning. Teaching multiple skills at once means multiple skills can be assessed at once making it time efficient (Oxford, 2001; Tajzad & Ostovar-Namaghi, 2014). Furthermore, focusing on a single skill at a time is not as authentic or natural compared to using multiple skills together since communication requires at least a mixture of two skills (Kebede, 2013; Oxford, 2001; Su, 2005; Tajzad & Ostovar-Namaghi, 2014). Students have reported that they prefer an integrated skills approach over a segregated skills approach as it can be used with authentic inputs to increase learners' language exposure, motivation, interest and confidence while also reducing stress (Lidawan & Alshlowi, 2020; Mekheimer, 2011; Pardede, 2019; Su, 2005; Tajzad & Ostovar-Namaghi, 2014).

Four strands approach online

Nation's (2007) four strands approach suggests language can be taught by focusing on four specific areas: meaning-focused inputs, meaning-focused outputs, language focus, and fluency. Meaning-focused input involves students being exposed to the target language in order to understand the content, with meaning-focused output seeing students create language to express themselves. Both of these meaning-focused strands are less concerned with grammatical correctness and are more concerned with creating meaning. The language-focused strand concentrates on language accuracy, while the fluency strand helps students use the language faster.

These four strands are not separate entities and can intermingle with each other (Nation, 2007). For example, an activity could be both a fluency exercise and a meaning focused-output exercise. Technology and Web 2.0 have also granted increasing potential to the four strands as there are more possible resources to draw from (Nation & Yamamoto, 2012). In the four strands, the educator takes the role of a planner who provides opportunities for students to practice language (Nation & Yamamoto, 2012). Educators should aim to have a balance of meaning-focused inputs, meaning-focused outputs, language focus, and fluency built into their courses (Nation, 2007).

Student generated content can be combined with integrated skills approaches while also applying the four strands. This combination results in activities and projects where the students' outputs become other students' inputs, which can then be recombined into a new output in another language skill area. For example, a student's spoken output can become a second students' listening input. This chapter outlines several specific examples of how this can be achieved online.

Pedagogical Implementations

In order to smoothly make use of student generated content in ways that allow students to interact with each other's work requires several online resources. These include video recording and sharing software, a learner management system (LMS), and a word processor. The main resource used in the following example activities is Flipgrid, which functions as the video recording and sharing space. Flipgrid has many advantages for classroom use (see Gyeongsang National University School of Language Education Curriculum Committee, 2020). It is free for educators and learners. It allows video sharing between peers who can respond using video or written comments of their own. It can keep videos private and only viewable by the educator by turning moderation on. Most importantly, it provides a safe-harbor for students as entry is restricted to learners who have been provided with the correct email domain and URL link. It is also worth mentioning that videos are stored on Flipgrid's cloud storage and will not take up valuable space on the educator's devices, and that this external storage might need to be noted for parents or institutions in regards to specific educational institution ethical and policy practices.

The following activities were designed using the four strands (Nation, 2007) and the integrated skills approach as a framework with student generated content elements. All of these projects require the use of an LMS and software for creating and hosting videos. We used Google Classroom and the LMS along with Flipgrid for video creation, storage and viewing.

The Four Skills Project

The four skills project integrates four language skills – speaking, listening, reading and writing – to create an integrated approach. This project was further designed to place emphasis on meaning-focused inputs and outputs in line with Nation's (2007) four strands. There are two parts to this project that aim to reduce the cognitive load on students and seek to divide the inputs and outputs in order to balance use of receptive and productive skills. In part one, students are given a graded reading as an input (provided by the instructor) and they must transform it into a student generated video advertisement as output. The advertisements must contain relevant information from the reading. These student generated outputs then become input during part two, as students watch the videos on Flipgrid, find the relevant information within them and generate a new written output using the information that they have discovered.

Through this project, students engage with authentic English and non-standard English to complete a multi-step project and demonstrate their ability to read, speak, listen and write as well as understand inputs and create outputs. We will use the topic of travel in our example.

For this example, educators will need to prepare authentic texts for the first input. These authentic texts should contain roughly the same information and be graded to an appropriate level for the class. For example, the activity we detail contains a travel theme so readings about 28 different travel resorts were gathered and modified to have a seventh to ninth grade reading level. Each reading contains specific information about the location of a resort, the price, what kind of people the resort is good for, and the various activities that can be undertaken while staying at the resort.

Part one

Students are each assigned an authentic text about a travel resort by the educator. Students read and discern the key information from the text. The key information includes the price, location, resort name, targeted travelers and the activities available to guests. This key information is then transformed into a travel advertisement video. The travel advertisement video is then recorded, either directly in Flipgrid or in a secondary editing program, before upload to Flipgrid.

Students can be evaluated on their language form, presentation skills, video quality as well as the correctness of their key information (reading comprehension). It can be beneficial to instruct students on paraphrasing and summarizing in previous classes to help students avoid plagiarism. Requiring students to use targeted vocabulary and grammar patterns can also help avoid plagiarism (Aguiar, 2020; Shiosaki & Aguiar, 2020). A prefabricated, and pre-provided rubric may assist students in following these particular guidelines.

Part two

Once the videos have been uploaded on Flipgrid, students view their peers' videos and identify the key information found within it. Students can freely select the videos they prefer or, if necessary, be assigned a specific peer video. Once students have watched and identified the key information, they should imagine that they have gone on vacation and stayed at that particular resort, with the intent being that they now need to write a travel review of their stay. This could be a positive or negative review but must include the key information from the peer video they were assigned or chose. Evaluation can be undertaken by examining language form, adherence to genre, and correctness of key information (listening comprehension). Additional requirements, such as comparing two videos, will encourage students to watch and understand more than one video. Again, a rubric may assist in guiding students, and the teacher in identifying the required aims and outcomes for students in this part.

Four Skills Variant

If educators want to provide additional student generated content to the project, then students can begin to create reading material in response to the first input. In example, we will rely on the topic of everyday problems and infomercials. Here students can be told to write a forum post on the LMS (e.g., Google Classroom) in which they complain about an everyday problem. In our classes, students came up with many problems, such as it being too humid to dry clothes, the smell of cigarette smoke wafting into their apartments from outside or different floors due to poor construction, and in other cases it simply being too hot in summer.

Students were then tasked to find the important information from their peers' forum posts and use that information to generate a solution in the form of an invention, after which they were required to develop an infomercial style advertisement for their product. These forum posts were assigned to individual students to prevent students from choosing their own reading. The posts were not edited for grammar, as communicating a solution by working with the language students already know is the purpose behind the practice. From here, the project follows the original procedure outlined in the previous example. Learners watch other students' infomercials and write a review, just as if they had bought the product. Students can be assessed on their ability to find key information in the material, as well as their ability to create a relevant solution.

This project variant involves more creativity and abstraction separating each input. The reading input results in a solution output, not just a transformation of one type of advertisement to another, and the solution output after becoming an input results in a fictional review. However, it requires more time to scaffold the language for infomercials as well as time to generate the initial reading input.

Other Projects

Adding student generated content to assignments need not generate novel projects. It is possible to combine aspects of common assignments found in textbooks to create an activity that builds on prior student work. In addition, such topics allow for integrated language skills approaches to be applied as meaning-focused inputs and outputs.

This chapter will now introduce three such activities. These activities have two parts each. In the first part, students generate the content that will be interpreted in the second. Two of these activities, directions and student generated comparisons were previously described in Shiosaki (2020).

Weather and Planning

Weather forecasts and making plans are not only two common activities found in textbooks but also topics that relate to each other. They also require similar language forms, such as future tense and modals of possibility. This activity combines two textbook topics to create a student generated, integrated skills assignment.

Part one: Content generation

Students watch a weather forecast and complete a cloze activity to provide them with a model. They then generated their own three-day weather forecast videos using this model. These weather forecasts are then uploaded to Flipgrid and made visible to classmates.

Part two: Content interpretation

Students watch their classmates' videos and note the weather forecast. They then write a role-play in which two people make plans around this weather forecast. Students can be evaluated on their ability to identify and use the information from the forecast in their role-play.

Student Generated Directions

Even in the age of smart phones with GPS tracking, sometimes asking directions is still necessary— a city map will not help find the bathroom in a large building. It also is a good way to use imperatives and prepositions.

This activity requires students to create a map to use in their videos thus access to drawing software may be necessary in addition to an LMS and video software. Alternatively, students could use a map provided by the educator.

Part one: Content generation

Students create a map of a real or fictional location using drawing software. Students use their maps to give directions from a stated starting point to a secret destination. Students record themselves giving the directions while displaying their map image. These videos are posted to Flipgrid and made visible to the class.

Part two: Content interpretation

Students watch other student generated videos and report on the LMS which video they watched and where they think the final destination is located. This activity could then be marked for correctness or followed up with a relevant post-activity.

Student Generated Comparisons

These comparison activities encourage critical and organizational thinking while also teaching comparative language. This activity allows for students to work with a wide diversity of topics and methods of presenting (e.g., students could generate spoken monologues, role-plays, written diaries, or long essays).

Part one: Content generation

Students are given the schema relevant to the particular lesson. They then use this schema to create content. For example, students could create and record role-play dialogues about shopping and prices. These dialogues can then be uploaded to Flipgrid.

Part two: Content interpretation

Students are given a worksheet to help them collect relevant information from the student generated content developed by peers in part one. Educators can then select specific student outputs, assign the students different outputs, or allow students to choose one from among all of the outputs available. Students should then read example comparison sentences, generate a few with educator assistance, then write their own. These comparisons should focus on content and meaning of the student generated content rather than delivery or correctness. These sentences can be submitted on the LMS and evaluated by the educator.

Notes/Observations

From implementing these activities and projects over two online semesters, there are some important observations that we have found noteworthy to mention pertaining to SGCs and integrated activities. First, students need a clear standard to work towards. The students seem to perform better when they can see examples of what is expected prior to the task. Interestingly, the students also use each other's products as standards. Thus, when videos are uploaded onto Flipgrid, students use these early completions as benchmarks for their own work. Similarly, students tend to gravitate towards student generated inputs that makes it easier to complete their next output. On Flipgrid, this can be observed by looking at the number of views a video has accumulated. For example, if a student created a very fine and clear video advertisement for the four skills projects, many students will choose to write their travel reviews using that particular video. This tendency from students is helpful as it verifies the quality of the work. Additionally, SGC helps students interact with their peers online as they view and respond to each other's content. This can help mitigate the feeling of isolation that can accompany taking classes only via online means. Students also respond more positively to activities involving SGC, regardless to the means of class delivery.

From Online to Offline

In some ways the online classroom is ideal for student generated content— students must have access to the internet, a sufficiently powerful device and, in most cases, access to a LMS and spaces to store their content. Additionally, because the online classroom exists in a virtual environment students and educators can easily move between these digital spaces.

However, while the online classroom is ideal for student generated content, the physical classroom is where it started. After all, prior to the current pandemic situation and a move to emergency remote teaching, classes were held primarily in physical spaces. In such a space student generated content has been implemented via databases of student questions (Luxton-Reilly et al., 2012), comic books (Morrison et al., 2002) among others.

The activities described in this chapter were designed for use in an online class, but they can be adjusted for use in the physical classroom. One possible option is to use a flipped classroom model for this purpose. Students would be expected to generate their initial output at home using their computers or other available devices. They would then bring that output to class where it would be used as an input. For example, students could generate weather forecasts at home. The educator would then show a selection in the classroom, and the students could generate their role plays with a partner in class. It could also be possible to treat the student generated content as entirely out of classroom content. Educators could spend the classroom time scaffolding activities leading to generating and responding to generated content. Then, students could complete both parts of the activities as homework.

It could also be possible to bring the advantages of a digital classroom into a physical one thanks to the increasing prevalence of smart phones, tablets, laptops and other mobile devices. Students could install the mobile versions of Google Classroom and Flipgrid on to their devices, and use them to create, submit and respond to student generated content during class. That is, if the use of such technologies is available due to administrative, and institutional policies. Moreover, by bringing the digital into the physical classroom, mixed environment activities become possible. For example, students could work more easily in groups to record their content, students could use the classroom for props, or the classroom itself could become the LMS for assigning and submitting content. Moving back to the physical classroom might bring challenges for student generated content, but it also brings with it perhaps new potential.

Conclusion

The recent COVID-19 pandemic forcing classes online provided a prime environment for the use of student generated content by teachers. As many of us now begin to move back into the physical or hybrid classroom, student generated content should continue to be applied whether this is through use of flipped classrooms or by employing mobile devices and applications with learners to bring some of the advantages of the digital classroom back into the physical one.

References

Aguiar A. (2020, July 14). *Solving online teaching problems through carefully designed tasks.* https://gnusle.com/2020/07/14/solving-online-teaching-problems-through-carefully-designed-tasks

Arguello, J.M. & Dempski, R.E. (2020). Fast, simple, student generated augmented reality approach for protein visualization in the classroom and home study. *Journal of Chemical Education, 97,* 2327–2331.

Arruabarrena, R., Sánchez, A., & Blanco, J.M. (2019). Integration of good practices of active methodologies with the reuse of student-generated content. *International Journal of Educational Technology in Higher Education, 16* (10). https://doi.org/10.1186/s41239-019-0140-7

Bates, S.P., Galloway, R.K., Riise, J., & Homer, D. (2014). Assessing the quality of a student-generated question repository. *Physical Review Physics Education Research, 10*(2) https://doi.org/10.1103/PhysRevSTPER.10.020105

Coulson, S. & Frawley, J. (2017). Student-generated multimedia for supporting learning in an undergraduate physiotherapy course. In H. Partridge, K. Davis, & J. Thomas. (Eds.), *Me, Us, IT! Proceedings ASCILITE2017: 34th International Conference on Innovation, Practice and Research in the Use of Educational Technologies in Tertiary Education* (pp. 235-244).

Dyson, L.E. (2012). Student-generated mobile learning: A shift in the educational paradigm for the 21st century. *anzMLearning Transactions on Mobile Learning, 1,* 15–19.

Gyeongsang National University School of Language Education Curriculum Committee. (2020, August 10). *Curriculum Committee Report Spring 2020.* https://gnusle.com/2020/08/10/curriculum-committee-report-spring-2020

Kebede, D. (2013). *The implementation of language skills integration in English as a Foreign Language (EFL) classes: Jimma College of Teachers' Education in focus* [Master's thesis, Jimma University College of Social sciences and Law, Ethiopia]. https://opendocs.ids.ac.uk/opendocs/handle/20.500.12413/6973

Ktoridou D. & Doukanari E. (2015). Student generated content in higher education technology-related blogs. In *2015 International Conference on Interactive Mobile Communication Technologies and Learning (IMCL)*, (pp. 289–295). IEEE.

Lee C. (2020). Question generation workflow: Incorporating student-generated content and peer evaluation [Unpublished thesis, Massachusetts Institute of Technology, USA]. https://dspace.mit.edu/handle/1721.1/127480

Lee, M. J., & McLoughlin, C. (2007). Teaching and learning in the Web 2.0 era: Empowering students through learner-generated content. *International Journal of Instructional Technology and Distance Learning, 4*(10), 21–34.

Levis, J. M., & Grant, L. (2003). Integrating pronunciation into ESL/EFL classrooms. *Tesol Journal, 12*(2), 13–19.

Lidawan, M. W., & Alshlowi, A. S. (2020). Authenticity and digital taxonomy for pragmatic integrative call through three approaches: Teachers' perspectives. *Journal of Linguistics, 4*(1), 15–29.

Luxon-Reilly, A., Denny, P., Plimmer, B., & Sheehan, R. (2012). Activities, affordances and attitude — How student generated questions assist learning. In *ITiSCE: Proceedings of the 17th ACM Annual Conference on Innovation and Technology in Computer Science Education*, (pp. 4–9). Association for Computing Machinery.

McLoughlin, C. & Lee, M.J.W. (2010). Personalised and self regulated learning in the Web 2.0 era: International exemplars of innovative pedagogy using social software. *Australasian Journal of Educational Technology, 26*(1), 28–43.

Mekheimer, M. (2011). Effectiveness of an integrated, holistic pedagogy of EFL skills in college students. *The Educational Research Journal, 25*(100), 41–74.

Morrison, T.G., Bryan, G., & Chilcoat, G.W. (2002). Using student-generated comic books in the classroom. *Journal of Adolescent & Adult Literacy, 45*(8), 758–767.

Nation, P. (2007). The four strands. *Innovation in Language Learning and Teaching, 1*(1), 1–12. https://doi.org/10.2167/illt039.0

Nation, P., & Yamamoto, A. (2012). Applying the four strands to language learning. *International Journal of Innovation in English Language Teaching, 1*(2), 167–181.

Oxford, R. (2001). Integrated Skills in the ESL/EFL Classroom. *ERIC Digest*, ED456670.

Pardede, P. (2019). Integrated skills approach in EFL classrooms: A literature review. In the *Proceedings of the English Education Department Collegiate Forum, Indonesia, Jakarta (pp. 147-149)*. UKI Press.

Persada, S.F., Ivanovski, J., Miraja, B.A., Nadlifatin, R., Mufidah, I., Chin, J., & Redi, A.A.N.P. (2020). Investigating generation Z' intention to use learners' generated content for learning activity: A theory of planned behavior approach. *International Journal of Emerging Technologies in Learning, 15*(4), 179–194. https://doi.org/10.3991/ijet.v15i04.11665

Pirhonene, J. & Rasi, P. (2017). Student-generated instruction videos facilitate learning through positive emotions. *Journal of Biological Education, 51*(3), 215–227. https://doi.org/10.1080/00219266.2016.1200647

Pysarchyk, O. L., & Yamshynska, N. V. (2015). The importance of integrating reading and writing for the EFL teaching. *Advanced Education, 3*, 77–83.

Shiosaki, N. & Aguiar A. (2020, November 26). *Making rubrics.* Gyeongsang National University, School of Language Education Workshop. https://gnusle.com/2020/11/26/making-rubrics

Shiosaki, N. (2020). Using technology to make listening more interactive. In D. Kent (Ed.), *Reimagining languaging: The future of education and teaching* (pp. 46–61). KOTESOL DCC.

Su, Y. C. (2005). Student Perceptions of the Integrated-Skills Approach in Taiwan's EFL College Classes. *Proceedings of the 13ᵗʰ Annual KOTESOL International Conference* (p. 125). KOTESOL.

Tajzad, M., & Ostovar-Namaghi, S. A. (2014). Exploring EFL Learners' Perceptions of Integrated Skills Approach: A Grounded Theory. *English Language Teaching, 7*(11), 92–98.

Wheeler, S., Yeomans, P., & Wheeler D. (2008). The good, the bad and the wiki: Evaluating student-generated content for collaborative learning. *British Journal of Educational Technology, 39*(6), 986–995. https://doi.org/10.1111/j.1467-8535.2007.00799.x

Yang X., Guo, X., & Yut, S. (2016). Student-generated content in college teaching: Content quality, behavioural pattern and learning performance. *Journal of Computer Assisted Learning, 32*, 1–15. https://doi.org/10.1111/jcal.12111

5. Defense of Social Justice in Education

Cyril Reyes
Woosong University

Abstract

In response to the recent COVID-19 pandemic and social and political discord, I clarify the moral and political justification for applying social justice ideas in education, by defining the moral obligation of educators in regard to social and political issues today. The need for clarification on this subject derives from the conflation of social justice and political correctness, which reduces the moral substance of social activism to censorship and cultural policing. This paper then, is not only a defense of social justice in education but provides a conceptual framework to separate the moral duty from the combative nature of political discourse. This conceptual framework is discussed through three specific positions: 1) a strong belief in social justice, 2) that of ambivalence, and 3) that of being uncomfortable with politics. Each of these positions is then defined by their specific political and non-political stances along with their respective moral justifications and what this means for those teachers that may adhere to such perspectives.

Recent skepticism has been expressed when ideas of social justice and political activism are applied in the field of education. Popular psychologist Jordan Peterson has been a vocal critic of social justice, and he has inspired reactionaries to discourage educators from expressing any claims of social justice, especially in higher education. As a staunch defender of hierarchical systems and the unequal outcomes produced by human interactions, Peterson defends the current social order when he describes how unequal social orders can be seen in crustaceans. In a video interview, Peterson explains:

> *I talk about crustacean hierarchies and simple crustacean nervous and our nervous system which a quite number of remarkable similarities. And the point isn't that we should behave like lobsters, of all the idiotic criticisms. It's that there's neurobiological continuity that demonstrates that hierarchies are so ancient that our brains have adapted to them, as if they are permanent elements of reality* (Peterson in Stossel & Lott, 2018).

If we follow Peterson's perspective, we should stay clear of social activism; instead, everyone should learn and listen to the traditional code that creates and maintains the hierarchy we find ourselves in. Social justice activism, in its attempt to dismantle the inherited inequities created by traditional societies, is a serious threat to the established order. Peterson states that "social justice courses on campuses change the meaning of the word 'justice' from rightfulness or lawfulness into a demand for justice for groups, based on the assumption each group must be equal to every other" (Peterson in Stossel, 2018 ¶,17). Further, Peterson has presented political correctness as the moral substance of social justice, one that permeates the ethos of radical leftism that infects the minds of young people today, taking a stance that I consider to further demoralize people from aspiring to think of social justice. This what I refer to as a disease in Peterson's and other conservative thinkers' minds is perhaps one of an existential threat, not just to higher education but the future stability of social relations. However, such criticism of social activism is not limited to conservatives. For many, political correctness has perhaps become a pejorative term. It defines a new type of censorship that encourages conforming to established, but narrow liberal morals. The critiques of this find support from radical leftists like Slavoj Zizek. He believes that political correctness is a form of cultural policing, which is an inauthentic form of interaction. We stop taking risks when conversing with others, by embodying the false politeness. Zizek argues that this form of political correctness is a desperate reaction to solve racism by controlling speech but fails to solve economic inequalities and social misunderstandings (Hendricks, 2019). Although I disagree with Zizek's interpretation that political correctness has led us to a new type of censorship, his statement characterizes how conservatives reduce social justice as an extension of a pervasive form of censorship. From this stance, there is a danger now that social justice is reduced to the type of false, inauthentic politeness that Zizek describes. More gravely, social justice as interpreted by Peterson may discourage educators from taking up social justice issues.

This chapter, as a classical apology for social justice in education, asserts that it is in schools that we can create spaces for debate, friendly disagreement, and critical discussion. This clarifies and defends the moral and political obligation of educators, with respect to those social and political issues that they and their students observe and experience. To this end, I discuss three specific positions: 1) a strong belief in social justice, 2) that of ambivalence, and 3) that of being uncomfortable with politics. With each perspective, I offer strategies and courses of action that can be applied based on the beliefs and assumption of that specific position. Each discussion clarifies the political and non-political stance of the relevant perspective as well as the moral justification associated with it. This defense, as the reader shall see, is not free from equivocation. I shall provide opposing points as to why a teacher should and should not take a social and political cause in their classroom, by separating the moral from the political, and delineating the conceptual and practical limits of both.

Right now, social justice issues are hard to ignore. The widespread effects of COVID-19 are especially felt by marginalized and disenfranchised groups (Jung, 2021). Reports have demonstrated that the current inequities are exacerbated by the pandemic's socio-economic impact (Kharas, 2020). These inequities have led to social unrest that began in the summer of

2020 with the call for racial justice in the United States; the rise of populism and anti-globalization movements offer regressive moral outlooks that resonate with people skeptical of the establishment. Above all else, from what I can see, misinformation is rampant in developed nations, undercutting feelings of solidarity and beliefs in democracy in nations that have been traditional pillars of liberal institutions and values.

These events and trends are in the news, but we also directly experience them. They are topics discussed outside of the classroom. Unlike past crises that had been taken for granted, ignored, dismissed, or underplayed, the COVID-19 pandemic has changed the global landscape in such a way that the effects of the pandemic have affected everyone. The question therefore is what should be done. What can educators exactly do particularly in relation to social justice?

Perspective # 1: A Strong belief in Social Justice
I teach my students with a strong belief that they must understand and agree with the tenets of social justice.

This is the perspective of someone who believes that education contains a mission to rectify historical errors, ameliorate suffering, and improve the human condition. This is a person who says: *I want my students to discuss why racism is wrong; I want them to investigate and research the growing wealth inequality and find connections between poverty and the effects of climate change.*

This position has the immediate danger of proselytizing to students. We begin with an idea that students must know X; they must care about X; they must hold these opinions concerning X; and they must act related to X. Such eagerness to improve the human condition conceals the fact that we must temper such enthusiasm with reality. It is easier and simpler to be indifferent to what others think is significant. For students, dismissing the importance of X is less complicated than understanding X and caring about X.

With this position, the best practice is not to preach about one's own social justice interests. For example, you may be motivated by the history of slavery and colonialism; such a teacher might present the recent cases of law enforcement and how these cases correlate with racist and discriminatory practices in the United States of America. Personally, I can certainly make the case to young people of the systemic injustice in America and other countries, and how such injustice is inseparable from socio-economic conditions. If taken, all of these options would amount to me lecturing, rather than asking my students about their own lived experiences that may very well include instances of injustice and inequality. My own social justice interests must give way to a higher imperative. *My students should choose their own social and political issue.* I should think of how my students will articulate their own concerns and fears of the relevant social problems that they have encountered. You might consider the question: *How can they express their own willingness to motivate others to improve their social condition as citizens?*

The social justice mission does not begin with the teacher. Students are citizens, and they participate in civil discourse; and they may be unconscious of the exact rights and duties that they have, yet they belong to the social and political world. In language classrooms around the world, each student brings a unique set of experiences that have a personal and public dimension. Some individuals might have taken great risks and endured terrible hardships to be where they are; some might be curious; some might not know what others in their class might have gone through. As tempting as it is to speak from a podium and lecture about world events, social justice as a pedagogical mission should begin with students having the opportunity to express themselves as citizens, so they can speak out about their own lived experiences. A social justice curriculum will have lessons designed for projects and papers that invite critical reflection and investigation of issues that students care about. As teachers who are enthusiastic about social justice, we invite the risk of political confrontation, but we must minimize conflict and misinformation. We ought to give students opportunities to test their research, expand on their investigation and reflect on the limits of their understanding, so they may imagine the possibilities that others have not yet thought about. Our classroom is a field of interaction for the creation of social justice projects. Our objective is not the propagation of a given social agenda; instead, it is creating the horizon of understanding that perpetuates thoughtful discussion and the investigation of an ethos appropriate for our times.

If we happen to have students who have been spared and privileged enough to avoid political oppression, racial injustice, or socio-economic inequalities, the right thing to do is not to make them feel guilty about their privilege. Everyone has a personal struggle; a personal story that we can learn from. Our students are not chess pieces in the game of politics or social affairs. As autonomous beings, students have their own desires, visions, and goals. All we can really do is help students navigate the continuum of social and political discourse and lend a hand as they chart their own course of action to bring their own vision of social change into reality.

Perspective # 2: Ambivalence

I want to believe in social justice, but I don't know where to start, and I'm afraid that talking about politics might create problems at work.

The second perspective is more common than the first. This is a person who believes in the moral precepts of social justice activism but has reservations. There is a good reason for this. Politics is divisive. Like competitive sports, politics encourages loyalty, fanaticism, and conflict. The confrontational nature of political discussion makes it a risqué topic in most social encounters. In the traditional settings of my culture, politics is a subject not to be discussed at the dinner table. Like religion, another taboo topic in polite company, politics is often seen as reserved for the obstinate and opinionated. In some ways, politics encourages us to have our biases confirmed, rather than listen to someone who doubts our beliefs. We then feel compelled to defend our biases and argue with strangers and family members for the sake of upholding our ideas. The question is why bother raising politics at all in the classroom when teachers and students need solidarity to create a functioning learning ecosystem. Because of its divisive nature, politics appears to be an unnecessary hindrance to the learning experience.

If you are uncomfortable about discussing political issues in your classroom because you are afraid of offending your employer and students, please remember that not all social issues are political. It is entirely possible to depoliticize the social discussion in your classroom by focusing on ethical and moral precepts of both your employer and/or students. The cultural and moral code of your employers and students transcend the public dimension; they are citizens, but they are also private individuals with expected moral obligations and duties. Appealing to national history and using historical narratives to contextualize social causes can unify groups of people. This is a great way to discuss social issues without igniting the ire of your employers and/or students. A present social issue or crisis may be compared to past historical events. Conflicts around the world compared to those that events precipitating theme, and to displaced people and refugee crises that have come before; despite the terrible events in history, atrocities create both victims and survivors. The fact that people in the short, but brutish history of humankind, have survived and endured is a testament to the durability of the human spirit; and we can galvanize enthusiasm for critical engagement for social discussion, by demonstrating how the world has significantly improved compared to the past. In a book full of tangible evidence of human flourishing, Rosling et. al

(2018, p. 61) describe the falling rates of child mortality, by contextualizing how deeply entrenched we are to see the world negatively:

> It is hard to see any of this global progress by looking out your window. Itis taking place beyond the horizon. But there are some clues you can tune into if you pay close attention. Listen carefully. Can you hear a child practicing the guitar or the piano? That child has not drowned and is instead experiencing the joy and freedom of making music.

When teaching social issues to students, begin with a unifying statement that draws on a positive affirmation of humanity, by highlighting progress made possible by ordinary people. We can circumvent controversial political issues by talking about transformations in the world today, and how each nation contributes or participates in the evolution of international affairs and the advancement of the sciences. For all our progress, there are still major obstacles and great dangers. Each citizen has a stake in policies and social causes related to the distribution of any fruits of scientific knowledge and the effects of global trade. The gaps created by globalization and technological advancement are beyond socio-political divisions; the consequences and effects of the fourth industrial revolution are structural to humankind (Harari, 2018). This type of conversation is of concern to us all, and the possible ways to reach non-abrasive and non-destructive outcomes in our future history requires a positive and inclusive dialogue that goes beyond past and present political divisions. We, as teachers, can collaborate with our students to initiate such a discussion about a better world that we can all envision.

Perspective #3: Uncomfortable with Politics.
I am not comfortable talking about social or political issues with my students.

This position is understandable, and perhaps even recommendable if you happen to be uncertain of your position on aspects of social justice, or you happen to believe that being agreeable is more important than advancing a social agenda, and of course an educator does not have to take up a political cause. Social activism in education requires the privilege of security. In some parts of the world where citizens attempt to exercise their right for civil obedience, that very right is considered a crime. Such teachers, under political duress, must find creative ways to resist the oppressive forces impinging on the classroom if they choose to take up a cause, and doing so without clandestine means would see such individuals punished by death or imprisonment. Living under an oppressive regime, an educator who believes in social justice takes a serious risk by speaking out. It is no different from being a journalist who speaks truth to power; an advocate who confronts an oligarch about wealth inequality; or standing in line in a protest. To require that everyone, or more specifically, that every educator, undertakes such a risk is not only unrealistic but irresponsible. Not everyone is equipped with the moral will to rise against power and to speak against the dominant forces in their society. Political advocacy is not a moral obligation that we can require of our students, of others, and especially ourselves, insofar as our moral actions have a separate dimension of individual and private choice. Moral imperatives are irreducible to the political. Even though political and moral lines may intersect, as educators, it is enough that we are engaging, sincere, respectful, and thoughtful in regard to our students, and to satisfy the civic and moral requirements of a good teacher in the societies in which we teach.

With that said, there are three complications that arise by taking a neutral stance in today's global political climate. The first is that the truth is under attack. Digital platforms have inadvertently paved the way for misinformation and confirmation bias, not only in political discussions, but even basic facts may be difficult to establish. It is as if there are now diverse ecosystems of knowledge and opinion, some of which permit the fabrication of facts, or worse, provide financial incentives for chicanery and bad faith (D'Ancona, 2017). Increasingly, the course of action taken by major institutions and private corporations is to censor sources and individuals spreading misinformation. The problem with censorship is that we reinforce the balkanization of the internet, rather than finding ways to establish solidarity and generate positive social capital through it. We live in a time where we can choose our own truths. Because of that, education is increasingly needed since objectivity and the veracity of truths and facts are in question. Dialogue and understanding are essential for a functional society; and teachers have an important role to play here. We can equip our students with better social media skills and implore the need for rigorous epistemic systems to scrutinize assertions and statements that they encounter on social media. Without engendering a respect for honesty and the ability to recognize and address the facts at hand with our students, we are perhaps not teachers but mere propagandists.

The second complication is that our students may in fact want to address a political point and we are unprepared to discuss it. This is a specific complication that may vary with respect to circumstance and location. In many affluent and democratic institutions, the politicization of the classroom mirrors the combative clamor we see on the nightly news and listen to over talk radio. If a teacher is not comfortable having a similar condition in his or her classroom, the best solution is to find appropriate resources on campus, so that students may avail themselves of an outlet to voice their concerns and their opinions. At the very least, we can engage specific students with strong beliefs, by hearing and listening to their opinions, and reserving judgment with respect to the content of their statements. The worse reaction is to draw swift conclusions about our students' political expression; our discomfort about an issue may very well derive from our own lack of knowledge. Our students may cross the line when voicing their opinions, perhaps at an inappropriate time, or may use strong language to make their point. However, we should reserve judgment as a collective body in the classroom. As educators we are moderators and facilitators of the dialogues in our classes. If we only play the role of arbiter, our discomfort about certain political stances may serve our ends, but perhaps then at the detriment of our students' spirit. To put it simply, there is no moral obligation for us to speak politically, but we do have the moral obligation to respect our students' opinions. We ought to manifest a model of behavior which sincerely engages with students' concerns, from both compassion and humanity.

The third complication is that social and political issues often enter the classroom as an elephant in the room. Recent crises produced by the pandemic are perhaps amplifications of deep structural problems in. societies globally. We may feel anxious and frightened when politics is debated in a public setting on campus, or at a private dinner party; and yet the fact that people voice their concerns about these issues and problems reveals that we do not have control over the mood of the conversation taking place before us. Everyone might desire a different subject to think about and discuss, but we cannot escape the news directly affecting us. The emergence of the COVID-19 pandemic has made it almost impossible for students and teachers to not talk about politics. There are social and political forces that shape how the pandemic is managed; the psychological toll of social distancing is being expressed by millions of people across social media. The language of grievance and frustration is inescapable, and to not address what is on everyone's minds is almost inhuman. We do not have to talk about social and political problems every class. Yet, to make it a rule to never discuss politics at all requires repressive and coercive strategies and tactics, and a willful ignorance to deny reality. By not speaking up, we normalize crises and socio-political issues, as if ignoring present social problems will make them disappear. Or worse, these social problems may become structural, inherent, and unchangeable. The attitude here being those of: we cannot do anything about them, so we should not talk about them; solutions are outside of educational institutions, thus outside of the classroom. If we follow this precept, we encourage the status quo and diminish the spirit of inquiry that is fundamental to education. It may demoralize the social bonds between individuals and citizens if we forbid classroom discourse from involving risks in speech. We surrender the responsibilities and duties of citizens to participate in civil discourse, with the justification that the classroom is not fit for such topics. If we accept the parameters laid out by anti-social justice activists and the suggestions by some employers, political silence practiced as normalization reduces students and teachers to spectators. As spectators, we can only glance at world events and pretend that our interaction in the classroom has no bearing on any crises unfolding around in our society.

Finally, with these three complications stated, I will reiterate their justification. The defense of social justice in education requires an understanding of different positions, and perhaps even defending the unconscious and unspeakable tenets of positions that we personally disagree with. Paradoxically, such a defense includes a recognition of the reasons why a teacher can choose to not take a political stand, to be silent, and to be a spectator. It is enough that we engage with other students as human beings, to respect them as persons with their own choices to make. It is not morally required that we should join our students and take up arms for a greater cause or to preach to them about a cause that they should care about. Social justice projects begin with them.

Conclusion

The three perspectives I have discussed here are not exhaustive of the different stances related to education and social justice. This paper offers strategic responses to the question of what teachers can do in their classroom with respect to social and political issues. My first suggestion is that believers of social justice should begin their projects and lessons with their students in mind. Students are not receivers of information; they are agents of their own social calling; storytellers of struggles they have experienced or witnessed. The second position is to rethink political discussion without the combative toxicity we see in popular media, by utilizing positive and unifying narratives that appeal to the moral core of humanity. The last position is a moral reflection that political advocacy is not for everyone; that there is no moral obligation to make social justice an issue in our classroom, and that student voice should not be stifled as it can be expressed in other ways. Finally, despite the complications that I have enumerated in this third perspective, it is not morally necessary for teachers to advocate for social justice; a teacher does not have to take a political stand, even if there are incredibly good reasons to do so.

References

D'Ancona, M. (2017). *Post-truth: The new war on truth and how to fight back*. Ebury Press.

Harari, Y. (2018). *Homo deus: A brief history of tomorrow*. Harper Perennial.

Hendricks, S. (2019, August 20). *Why Slavoj Zizek thinks political correctness is dumb*. Big Think. https://bigthink.com/politics-current-affairs/slavoj-zizek-political-correctness

Jung, M. (2021, February 01). COVID-19 contributed to widening of income inequality: BOK. *The Korea Herald*. http://www.koreaherald.com/view.php?ud=20210201000878

Kharas, H. (2020, October 21). The impact of COVID-19 on global extreme poverty. The Brookings Institution. https://www.brookings.edu/blog/future-development/2020/10/21/the-impact-of-covid-19-on-global-extreme-poverty

Rosling, H., Ronnlund, A., & Rosling, O. (2018). *Factfulness: Ten reasons we're wrong about the world – and why things are better than you think.* Flatiron Books.

Stossel, J. (2018, June 13). *Jordan Peterson vs. the Left.* Reason: Free Minds and Free Markets. https://reason.com/2018/06/13/jordan-peterson-vs-the-left

Stossel, J., & Lott, M. (2018, June 19). *Political Correctness. Stossel: Jordan Peterson vs. 'Social Justice Warriors'* [video]. Reason: Free Minds and Free Markets. https://reason.com/video/2018/06/19/stossel-jordan-peterson-vs-social-justic/?itm_source=parsely-api

6. Communicating with Students in the Korean Classroom – Crossing the Cultural Barrier (Preconceptions and Cultural Differences)

Retha Choi
Woosong Information College

Abstract

There are a couple of important questions that can be raised when thinking about communicating with English language students in the Republic of Korea (hereafter Korea). To begin with, why is it important to communicate clearly between the teacher and these students? Secondly, what kind of cultural and permanent misunderstandings can occur between the teacher and these students? Clear communication is required in order to provide a great teaching experience for students as miscommunication may occur due to an inappropriate use of verbal and non-verbal cues which can then lead to cultural misunderstandings. This may then result in the student becoming anxious and consciously or subconsciously then not responding to the teacher. Educators should also limit their use of jargon, idioms, sarcasm, or academic words, as these might confuse uninformed students. Negative biases and cultural differences between teachers and students are also considered in classroom communication in this chapter. Here, students may have separate ways of learning that are at odds to the teacher's learning ideals and biases, which can then lead to poor communication through verbal cues, preconceptions, and cultural differences. The first step for teachers is to acknowledge these problems and take a few simple steps to reduce them. This can be achieved by establishing a a good rapport, showing empathy, and by being aware of verbal and nonverbal cues. Also, be aware of any use of confusing or intimidating language and actions until students get used to your teaching style. As well, use open-ended questions to let students know that care is being given for their feedback. This chapter will also explore these issues and expand on ways to implement them in the classroom through a flipped classroom pedagogical approach and through the author's experiences of teaching in Korea both before and during the COVID-19 pandemic. Some implications for post-pandemic teaching going forward emerge.

Introduction

This chapter will address the challenges faced by a teacher instructing students in Korea in the English language classroom in terms of communication. It will address questions of verbal and non-verbal communication and cultural misunderstandings that may arise as a result. Preconceptions from the teacher and students and cultural differences can lead to misunderstandings in the classroom. It will address what a teacher can do to name these problems and to mitigate communication problems between themselves and their students through self-assessment. It will also develop ideas of best communication practice utilizing Zoom and the classroom developed from the author's 25 years of teaching experience in Korea, and these will be based on personalized learning (flipped classroom), gamification, and combining traditional and nontraditional concepts of teaching.

Verbal and nonverbal communication – Direct and Indirect Communication

What is verbal and non-verbal communication? It is spoken or verbal communication which includes face to face, telephone, radio and television, and other media. Nonverbal communication is body language, gestures, the way we dress or act, where we stand, and even what we smell (Skills You Need, 2021). Verbal and non-verbal communication connects with direct and indirect communication. In most Western cultures, communication occurs in a way where they want to get the message across to others directly in the classroom, while in most Asian cultures indirect communication views the teacher as the most indispensable one in the communication.

Every culture has its own versions of verbal and nonverbal cues or communication. People use their nonverbal cues in diverse ways, for example in one culture "men are socialized to be in control, to have and exercise authority" (Nelson, 2020, ¶1). In most Western cultures people of any gender identity believe that authority in the classroom is necessary. However a foreign teacher who comes across this way, this is intimidating to Korean students. It can lead to anxiety and they will not speak in class. Korean students are used to only listening to the teacher, they have not been allowed or taught to speak up in the classroom by their Korean teachers. My thought here is that foreign teachers need to be less authoritarian and more empathetic and understanding toward their learners as a result of where they have come from and this past learning/teaching experience. However, there should be a fine line between being strict and too lenient. Being kind and empathetic is not something that should be overlooked when teaching anywhere, but in Korea, I have always seen and felt it very well received by students. So too, effective communication uses context. In other words, how the message is delivered, and how it is heard (Katz, 2020). Learning to read your students' actions and reactions in the classroom is part of empathy. Through taking an interest in the students as people rather than as a commodity, this will help the teacher to help learners to express themselves in the classroom.

A teacher needs to be aware of their own body language and learn certain cultural taboos when teaching in a Korean classroom. Korean students will not use direct eye to eye contact, because it is a sign of disrespect to the teacher. However, in Western societies, a student is generally expected to look directly in the eye of a teacher. The teacher must be aware of this (IEC, 2021) and realize that forms of indirect communication are the most often used in Korea and other Asian countries. The students are very observant of the teachers' body language, posture, tone of voice, and facial expressions. The teacher should be aware of how the students will also communicate nonverbally. Indirect communication is a form of communication that will help these learners in saving face and creating a harmonious classroom atmosphere, indirect communication should be, counteracted with open-ended questions, which is discussed later. Direct versus indirect communication can cause miscommunication. The teacher should become aware of the differences. When the teacher works with the students being conscious of the differences and is sensitive enough to show that understanding as they teach, it will make an immense difference. See table 1 for the differences between direct versus indirect communication.

Table 1

Direct vs. Indirect Communication (based on IEC, 2021)

Direct Communication	Indirect Communication
The aim is to be clear and honest.	The aim is to keep things harmonious.
Words are fundamental.	Non-verbal language is employed.
The message is of the utmost importance.	The person with the message is indispensable.
Comfortable in confrontational situations.	Avoid a situation where there is confrontation.

In the English language classroom students will often take time to answer a question to formulate it and to make sure that they can say it correctly. As a teacher, we should not hold them to quick, unthought out answers. Give them time to formulate and even work together to share an answer they feel is thoughtful and correct. That is why group work in the Korean classroom can work well. Often in Western society, individual answers are the normal rhetoric, and students may also volunteer such answers.

However, because students in the Korean classroom often have a group mentality, seeing students work together is really a good model to use such an environment. Group work then is the best and can have a profound effect on each student. For example, as students start working together and the teacher is consistently using a routine in their teaching, students are apt to catch on to the teacher's way of speech and classroom expectations if they use group work methods. This can then relieve student's anxiety of confronting the teacher face to face when working individually and one-on-one, thus making students more likely to open up, as the teacher monitors group activities.

Group activities like games, worksheets, and many other means of working together is an effective way to help students to learn from each other, with students adapting to group activities (McClure, 2007). Consistent use of groups and making the curriculum and procedures the same, can help students learn how to communicate and feel more at ease with the teacher in the classroom.

Limit Jargon, and Sarcasm.

Educated professionals that come to Korea or come from other countries may not have teacher training. They may come from a variety of educational backgrounds and vary from those who are coming back out of retirement through to those who have just come fresh out of college. These people then begin life as a teacher, unfortunately lacking professional skills for teaching ESL/EFL pupils, and most end up teaching themselves how to get along. This may see biases emerge. When instructing students learning English, it is easy for teachers to use vernacular phrases, sarcasm, and perhaps too academic jargon. It is confusing for a student who is new to a language or culture if the teacher is not adjusting their speech styles to the level of the classroom. Often, the teacher may try to teach from his own prejudices and use jargon from their previous field(s) of study. It may make it more difficult for students to understand and relate to the instructor. For those of us who are trained teachers, we should also be aware of such issues, as parents and the public may not understand the theory or ideas that educators understand and be readily able to discuss them. Also, as Poedjosoedarmo (2005) reminds us, communication breakdowns often occur during cross-cultural communication as a result of interlocutor differences in cultural perspectives. As such, teachers must learn to reduce academic jargon, reduce the use of vernacular expressions and sarcasm, until students become more familiar with the expressions or the teachers' background and teaching methods. Students will laugh when they think that they should, but this is often a nervous response rather than a humorous one, particularly as the Western use of sarcasm may be misunderstood in a Korean classroom. As students learn to understand the teacher and follow instructions in English, many will notice and understand sarcasm. They will learn eventually, but it can take a lot of time. Sarcasm in general then, should be minimized.

Perhaps, teachers should take the advice of Mahatma Gandhi here, and begin to learn from your students, realize that they are educated and capable of learning another language.

> *A teacher who establishes rapport with the taught becomes one with them, learns more from them than he teaches them. He who learns nothing from his disciples is worthless. Whenever I talk with someone, I learn from him. I take from him more than I give him* (Gandhi, in Mishra, 2015, p. 325).

Students will learn, but teaching takes patience from instructors. Instructors will have to be creative, empathetic, and grow in their own skills.

Negative Preconceptions and Cultural Differences- CQ or Cultural IQ

A teacher from a Western culture may want to enter the Korean classroom with knowledge of the students' cultural backgrounds.

In other words, the teacher should have intercultural competence (DeJaeghere & Zhang, 2008), this is developed through research of the cultures and eventually through experience. A teacher with competence in intercultural understanding can become a teacher that can teach with empathy. The teacher needs to learn to develop their cultural quotient (CQ) or cultural intelligence quotient (cultural IQ) (Triandis, 2004). CQ was conceptualized by Earley and Soon in 2003 (Soon & Van Dyne, 2008). This is often developed when the teacher learns the language of the other culture in which they reside, or through work experience within another culture (Earley & Soon, 2003), and by living in diverse cultures (Triandis, 2004). The more a teacher has such lived experience, the higher their cultural IQ will become. It is necessary then for a teacher to open themselves up to innovative ideas and thoughts. By understanding the culture, they live in, the easier it will be to show consideration and understanding of the students who go to class within that culture.

How does CQ communicate through Zoom or other digital avenues of teaching? This is an important question, particularly in times of emergency remote teaching, and in moving forward with hybrid classes. Communicating with students on Zoom and in the classroom at the same time, when conducting hybrid teaching, is often a great learning experience for the teacher. A show of empathy and CQ is particularly important here, as teachers may be introduced into the student's home, bedroom , or communal living space. How do students react? How do teachers react? Again, empathy is something a teacher should use and not be as strict as they may be in a face-to-face setting. Developing a united curriculum for these spaces (Zoom and classroom combined) will see a teacher need to work harder to converge the two dynamics of each teaching environment. A teacher will have to dig deep into their creativity to develop ways to make the experience interesting both groups of students. The teacher's expectations of the students should be the same as if they were in the classroom yet the teacher should be understanding enough to not be policing the students all of the time. The teacher might wish to make their curriculum a mixture of traditional activities alongside those based on gamification in order to keep students focused on the concept that is being taught.

If the teacher is teaching on Zoom and in the classroom at the same time, use of the breakout rooms in the online space can be used while face-to-face students work in groups. Making a pair on Zoom work with a pair in the classroom, forming a group of four, where activities are completed using the learners mobile phones. That is if the institutional ethical, privacy, and technology procedures allow for such use. The teacher is then able to move within the classroom and into the breakout rooms on Zoom while maintaining social distancing if required. This also allows for students to interact with all members of the class, while providing more student talk time. As the teacher's CQ increases the teacher and the student's communication will improve. Teaching students of expected Zoom class etiquette and also classroom etiquette can help learners also understand and come to groups with teacher expectations (Table2 and table 3 provide examples.)

As you can see, the expected etiquette outlined is similar for both the Zoom and classroom contexts. Merging both sets of etiquette can help the teacher navigate hybrid teaching, while it also makes things also clear for students participating in the class from either modality. This is based on the author's experience while teaching through the pandemic and in such a context.

Table 2
Zoom Class Etiquette

Zoom Class Etiquette
- Be on time – Have your computer or phone ready before the class time.
- Presentation – Turn your video on. Be dressed nicely. Be in view of the camera.
- Mute Yourself – Turn off the microphone. Turn it on to speak.
- Headphones – Use headphones. It's easier to hear you.
- Participation – Be focused, attentive and an active participant. No cell phones.
- Chat Responsibly – Click the raised hand icon to speak. Type questions in the chat.
- Communication – Speak clearly. Look up when speaking. Stay on topic.
- Be Respectful – Be kind and considerate.

Table 3
Classroom Etiquette

Classroom Etiquette
- Be on time – Come into the classroom before class time.
- No cheating-don't rely on other students to help you – Do it yourself.
- Attend every class – Attendance is necessary to complete the course.
- No private conversations – Talking while the professor or classmates are talking is distracting.
- Participation – Be focused, attentive and an active participant. No cellphones unless needed for classroom activities.
- Come to class prepared – Have all homework, readings and vocabulary studied before class.
- Turn in work on time – In the classroom or the learner management system (LMS), have assignments finished.
- Be respectful – Be kind and considerate.

Personalized Learning, Gamification, and Communication

Personalized learning, the term I use to refer to homework activities with my learners, that can be performed in and out of the classroom is a way for students to learn by themselves and to engage with co-learning with their classmates if they have finished all other work. Further, online games mixed with conventional classroom concepts can ease learning for the student. The author has successfully applied Kahoot! for many years. Lesson content, such as vocabulary, readings, and questions can be used in Kahoot challenges and provide a means of formative assessment. No matter the platform, the challenge is to provide learners with the ability to practice in a personal and fun way. Then, when they come to class they will succeed working with language while engaging in gamification. Game-based learning can help to engage students and consolidate vocabulary or the set readings for them. This also allows the teacher to use the vocabulary from the text in class, knowing that students have met those words previously, and that students already have an understanding of the material they will be working with during the lesson.

On the other hand, personalized learning is in line with that which can be delivered via a flipped classroom. This is an educational concept of learning that transfers the concept of learning to the individual (Flip Learning, 2014). Teachers are thus able to become guides in class, where they work to ensure that the learning developed by students outside of class is practiced and undertaken within the learning context. When students learn the material in their own time and surroundings, they are more likely to engage with it with more enthusiasm than they may in the face-to-face classroom or when in a Zoom class session. To see this work effectively, the aim is to combine group work with individual study. The author believes that with this approach, students will feel more at ease with the teacher with the approach helping the learner to feel more successful in their use of the language that they are learning. In such cases, the instructor may need to learn from trial and error, before they find how this can work most effectively for them and their learners with their CQ developing while doing so. As this occurs communication between the students and the instructor should become clearer and each will be able to learn from the other. In such a context then, collaboration and group learning becomes more effective and perhaps easier, both for the students and the teacher. See table 4 for a comparison of the traditional versus flipped classroom approach to teaching and learning.

Table 4

The Traditional Classroom vs. The Flipped Classroom (based on Flip Learning, 2014)

Traditional Classroom	**Flipped Classroom**
- Instructor stands between the student and knowledge. - Instructor is inflexible of expectations of timeline and assessment. - Instructor is the primary source of information. - Instructor is the primary source of information. - Instructor is the primary source of information.	- Students have direct access to the knowledge. - Instructor is more flexible in expectations of the timeline and assessment. - In class time is dedicated to more exploration and more in-depth study. - Instructor curates prioritizes and differentiate to make content accessible to all students. - Instructor makes themselves available to students; individually, small groups and gives classroom feedback.

The author has learned through trial and error how to run a flipped classroom environment and is still learning. This is a one-way CQ, from which communication can develop, and helps for all involved to solidify the concept that the student is the focus and not the instructor. From experience, students in the Korean classroom can then quickly learn and feel increasingly comfortable with the way that the teacher teaches, and how they can then work through any difficulties of learning another language and culture. As such, students become more open to working with the teacher and become more comfortable as this approach allows for the teacher to take higher interest in students and provide feedback that is of the type that they need, and so communication opens.

Open-Ended vs. Close Ended Questions
The use of open-ended and close-ended questions in the classroom is the last exemplar of good and bad communication. It is another example of how to get students to communicate better in the classroom if the instructor wants the students to take part communicatively when in the classroom (Tolzin, 2015). Open-ended questions are questions that ask what, why, and how. These kinds of questions open up the subject and allow the students to give their opinions, or examples based on their knowledge of the subject and to garner answers from their own experiences too. They feel as if the teacher really wants to know what they are thinking. On the other hand, close-ended questions stop conversations in their tracks as students might only give an answer that they think the teacher wants, or may answer with a single word such as 'yes', 'no', or 'maybe'.

If used, students will get used to the need to provide a complete sentence answer to open-ended questions. As the teacher develops such questions, they should always be aware of expected answers and be prepared for the kinds of answers they may want to receive or model for students. The educator should consider the previously mentioned concept of how most students in the Korean classroom communicate through indirect means, in this way the instructor can be more open to consider that teaching with open-ended questions will develop their learners ability to communicate better in the classroom. This can then assist students in developing a more direct way of communicating in the language that they are learning. Table 5 presents the differences between open- and closed-ended questions, along with what they should begin with, and some examples.

Table 5.

Open-Ended vs Closed-Ended Questions (based on Tolzin, 2015)

Open-Ended Questions	**Closed-Ended Questions**
Questions designed for a meaningful response based on a person's feelings, thoughts and knowledge.	A question which limits a person's choice of answers, usually with one-word answers, such as 'yes or 'no.
Begin with	*Begin with*
What ...? Why ...? How ...?	Is/are ...? Do/Did ...? Would/Will ...? Could/Can ...? Was/Were ...? Have/Has ...? Which ...? Who ...? When ...? Where ...?
Examples	*Examples*
1. How do you feel today? 2. What is your favorite memory from childhood? 3. Explain/How you would find that. 4. Why did that happen? 5. How do you get to work? 6. What happened in class?	1. Are you satisfied? 2. Did you find it? 3. Do you think you would use this? 4. Could you help me? 5. Were you happy? 6. Which one? 7. Who is the author?

Conclusion

In conclusion, we can answer the questions expressed about how important it is to learn to communicate with those learners that we as teachers will meet in the Korean classroom, and how we might avoid bias and miscommunication. This can be achieved through the educator's development of CQ, and in knowing how their individual learner's cultures communicate (e.g., through direct or indirect means), and by not forcing upon students their own biases. An educator, through self-assessment, limiting jargon and vernacular language, and by being aware of verbal and non-verbal cues, body language, preconceived notions, and cultural biases, can then become increasingly aware of the students' needs in the classroom. The educator will find that over-communicating, patience, empathy, and building a rapport with the students that they teach will in turn assist in communicating learner expectations. Students will, in turn, eventually become more open to speak in class and eventually learn a new way of communicating directly while using the language they are learning. In this chapter, a number of examples of means to be able to encourage this have been provided. Preparing in advance is an effective way of being able to communicate effectively with students. Various techniques, such as gamification, can be used to communicate to the students the aspects of lessons required for understanding the teacher and the material. Perhaps, prepare ahead of time weekly material on a set schedule that can be provided to learners through the learner management system that the workplace uses. Here, from experience, the author would allow a full week to introduce the curriculum and assess the personalized learning that is being implemented over the course. Keep in mind that using personalized learning may assist learners in consolidating the lesson in their memory as they access the learning content in various means. It is important too, that if you do find yourself in an online teaching session that you adopt the mindset of going to work. In this case, be professionally dressed and ready for the lesson, just as you would if teaching face-to-face. Also, be sympathetic to the home situation of each student and their contexts (e.g., Wi-Fi connection issues, communal spaces). You may also wish to consider the tips provided in table 6 if you find yourself teaching out of your home in the future. Above all, face-to-face or online, be empathetic and learn to over-communicate the lesson patiently utilizing a variety of communication pathways.

Table 6.

Tips for Teaching Classes from a Home Space (based on Canva, 2021).

Tips for Teaching Classes from a Home Space	
Prepare in Advance	- If you are planning to teach remotely in the near future, consult the curriculum and prepare lessons for the coming weeks. - Opt for content that can be easily accessed online, and through various mediums
Give Students Weekly Schedules on the LMS	- Allow students to prepare and study lessons in advance of class. They therefore know the subject matter and the vocabulary and expected discussions. - Plan time during the online session to review correct responses to content. - Allow one full week for one lesson, as you would in the normal face-to-face context.
Set up a Work Zone	- Create a comfortable and well-illuminated room, table, or area; designate a special workspace. - Dress professionally, and in line with employer guidelines. - Avoid working from the couch or bed, this may change the nature of that space for you while not working.

Create an Online Quiz	- Check in on your students' learning progress through online methods. - Use a tool like Google Forms or Kahoot to evaluate learner progress and engage in such application use during online sessions.
Over-Communicate	- Clearly establish your expectations through a variety of communication channels. - Ensure students know exactly where to receive content, submit their work, or ask questions. - Do not be afraid to repeat the instructions many times (e.g., on the LMS, via SMS, and again through an email or five.
Be Flexible	- Be empathetic of the home situation of students as some may not have available adult supervision or a reliable internet connection. - If students need special support, then be open to their unique needs.

As educators and students all over the world must grapple with how to go to school and work during a pandemic, being open to new ways of communicating, and being aware of each other's cultural differences and needs will go far in learning any new teaching strategies, methods, techniques, approaches, and activities that may be required. Breaking away from the traditional classroom methods and being pushed into emergency remote teaching, most of us without any support to do so, have had time to adapt and employ media, learner management systems, and new ways of teaching. Learning to collaborate with our learners, and being open to new ways of learning, will assist us in improving and supporting our teaching while working with students as teammates no matter the cultural background.

References

Bradford, A., Duval, M., Bachman, S., Mohess, D., Dort, J., & Kapadia, M. (2020). Building rapport and earning the surgical patient's trust in the era of social distancing: Teaching patient-centered communication during video conference encounters to medical students. *Journal of Surgical Education, 78.* https://doi.org/10.1016/j.jsurg.2020.06.018

Brown, T., Williams, B., Boyle, M., Molloy, A., McKenna, L., Molloy, L., & Lewis, B. (2010). Levels of empathy in undergraduate occupational therapy students. *Occupational Therapy International, 17*(3).

Canva. (2021). Distance education: Tips for teaching from home [Infographic]. https://www.canva.com/design/DAEXHa14B1g/iM2MEFmrX1Qj9Ix0bYR8AQ/view?utm_content=DAEXHa14B1g&utm_campaign=designshare&utm_medium=link&utm_source=homepage_design_menu

Courtenay-Hall, P. (2001). Review of environmental education for sustainability: Good environment, good life. *Canadian Journal of Higher Education, 31*(2).

DeCapua,Andrea E. (2016). *Crossing Cultures in the language Classroom* (2nd Ed.). University of Michigan Press.

DeJaeghere, J., & Zhang, Y. (2008). Development of intercultural competence among US American teachers: Professional development factors that enhance competence. *Intercultural Education, 19,*(3), 255-268.

Earley, P. C., & Soon, A. (2003). *Cultural intelligence: Individual interactions across cultures.* Stanford University Press.

Faranda, W. T., & Clarke, I. (2004). Student observations of outstanding teaching: implications for marketing educators. *Journal of Marketing Education, 26*(3), 271–281. https://doi.org/10.1177/0273475304268782

Farooq A, Rizwan S, Qureshi SF, Hassan U. (2020). Covid-19 the disruptor; Challenges and opportunities in medical education. *Isra Medical Jouranl, 12*(1), 34-41.

Flip Learning. (2014). *Definition of flipped learning.* Flipped Learning Network. https://flippedlearning.org/definition-of-flipped-learning

Han, S. (2004) Effective environments for English language learning and teaching in Korea: A study of adult EFL learners' perceptions [Doctoral dissertation]. Monash University, Australia.

Heeman K., & Zizi P. (2003) Cross-cultural differences in online self-presentation: A content analysis of personal Korean and US home pages. *Asian Journal of Communication, 13*(1), 100-119. https://doi.org/10.1080/01292980309364833

IEC. (2021). South Korean culture. *Cultural Atlas.* https://culturalatlas.sbs.com.au/south-korean-culture/south-korean-culture-communication

Jung, M. (2010). Korean university students' willingness to communicate. *Studies in English Language & Literature, 36*(1). 283-311. https://doi.org/10.21559/aellk.2010.36.1.015

Katz, L. S. (2020, August 8). 5 Essential Strategies for Effective Communication. *Psychology Today.* https://www.psychologytoday.com/us/blog/healing-sexual-trauma/202008/5-essential-strategies-effective-communication

Kim, J. Y. (2016). Group work oral participation: Examining Korean students' adjustment process in a US university. *Australian Journal of Adult Learning, 56*(3), 400–423.

Lawler, E. M., Chen, X. M., & Venso, E. A. (2007). Student perspectives on teaching techniques and outstanding teachers. *Journal of the Scholarship of Teaching and Learning, 7*(2), 32-48.

Lee, J. (2019). EFL students' views of willingness to communicate in the extramural digital context. *Computer Assisted Language Learning, 32,*(7), 1-21. https://doi.org/10.1080/09588221.2018.1535509

Mackay, B., DeCapua, A., & Wintergerst, A. (2004). Crossing Cultures in the Language Classroom. *TESOL Quarterly, 38*(4).

Mishra, A. (2015). *Mahatma Gandhi on Education*. Vikas Publishing.

Park, M. (2016) Integrating rapport-building into language instruction: A study of Korean foreign language classes, *Classroom Discourse,* 7,(2), 109-130. https://doi.org/10.1080/19463014.2015.1116103

McClure, J. (2007) International graduates' cross-cultural adjustment: Experiences, coping strategies, and suggested programmatic responses. *Teaching in Higher Education, 12*(2), 199-217. https://doi.org10.1080/13562510701191976

Neborsky, E., Boguslavsky, M., Ladyzhets, N., Naumova, T., & Anisimov, A. (2020). Transition to distance learning under COVID-19 in assessments by professors. *Perspectives of Science and Education,* 4(46), 99-110. https://doi.org/10.32744/pse.2020.4.6

Nelson, A. (2017, December 31). Men, Power and Nonverbal Cues. *Pyschology Today.* https://www.psychologytoday.com/intl/blog/he-speaks-she-speaks/201712/men-power-and-nonverbal-cues

Poedjosoedarmo, G. Cross-cultural communication: Linguistic and cultural dimensions – implications for the language classroom. *TEFLIN Journal, 16*(1) p. 26-41

Skills You Need. (2021). *What is communication?* https://www.skillsyouneed.com/ips/what-is-communication.html

Tolzin, T. (2015). *Open and close ended questions* [Video]. YouTube. https://www.youtube.com/watch?v=rdeuiXc4bG0

Triandis, H. (2004). The many dimensions of culture. *The Academy of Management Executive,* 18(1), 88-93. https://www.jstor.org/stable/4166039

Valenziano, K. B., Glod, S. A., Jia, S., Belser, A., Brazell, B., Dellasega, C., Duncan, L., Farnan, M., Haidet, P., Phillips, J., Wolpaw, D., & Dillon, P. W. (2018). An interprofessional curriculum to advance relational coordination and professionalism in early-career practitioners. MedEdPORTAL: The Journal of Teaching and Learning Resources, 14(10697). https://doi.org/10.15766/mep_2374-8265.10697

7. University LMS-based Wiki use with EFL Writing Students During Emergency Remote Teaching

Michael Cary
Kyonggi University – Suwon Campus

Abstract

This chapter discusses what wikis are and some key features regarding them. It briefly details the government guidelines for universities in the Republic of Korea starting the spring semester of 2020 during the emergence of COVID-19, and following this, the ways a university learner management system (LMS) wiki can be applied during emergency remote teaching (ERT) of online writing English as a foreign language (EFL) classes. A number of writing tasks that students were able to complete using such a system, and how these activities met the necessary instructional goals for the classes in which the students were enrolled are detailed.

Introduction to Wikis

The word wiki has become synonymous nowadays with one website, Wikipedia.org. However, wikis are more than just a website that many may visit to gain information about a topic. Most know that Wikipedia content is created and curated by multiple authors, and this is what sets a wiki apart from other websites. A key idea behind using a wiki is that multiple authors can contribute and curate information, as well as add multiple pages to the wiki as required. As such, wikis are websites that anyone can create, and add any user(s) they wish to, in order for multi-authored online content to be created. Some internet users join a wiki on their own without being invited or added as well.

There are a number of public and private/secure wikis available. Commercial wiki creation sites such as www.pbworks.com and those such as MediaWiki are available for download. The latter is what powers Wikipedia. Teachers and educators from all over the world have been coming up with ways to use wikis for the past decade (Richardson, 2009). Several universities, including ones in the Republic of Korea (hereafter Korea), have wikis embedded in their central webpages or have them available on their servers for faculty to use through the learner management system (LMS). Some universities such as Hanyang University in Seoul and Ansan, Korea make their university wiki visible to the public from their homepage (www.hanyang.ac.kr). Other universities such as Kyonggi University in Seoul and Suwon do not make a university wide wiki available to the public, but they do provide options to use a wiki through the university's LMS.

The type of wiki that an educator may choose to use depends on their goals or the needs that they might have for their particular classroom or learning environment. If an instructor's main goal is to teach about audience, and gaining exposure to an audience, then one may want to use a commercial wiki with public visibility. However, many teachers who teach English as a foreign or second language in Korea are primarily concerned with building confidence in the students' communicative abilities. Being able to limit the visibility of your students' work to only the other students in your class may be a good thing here. Determining what your teaching goals are for the class will be the main factor in the decision any teacher faces when working from within an online learning platform, and when selecting the type of wiki to use with their learners.

If your goals or class instruction primarily focus around getting students to speak and vocally produce the language that they are learning, then a wiki, even the best commercial one, may not be suitable. As an educator who has been working with wikis involving university students since 2008 (http://esln312.pbworks.com), I have found that wikis for EFL teachers in Korea may lend themselves best to achieving writing goals. As such, I apply wiki use within my writing skills-based classes rather than my speaking skills-based classes. It is also important for me as an educator to create rich and meaningful interactions in my classes every semester, and a wiki helps me to do this. Since wikis are by definition websites with multiple users/editors, they can easily facilitate collaborative learning as Dillenbourg (2000, p. 24) notes,

> *Simply stated, collaborative learning is effective if the group members engage in rich interactions: When they explain themselves in terms of conceptions and not simply answers, when they argue about the meaning of terms and representations, when they shift roles, … One cannot a priori guarantee that rich interactions occur, but one can regulate the collaborative process to favor the emergence of these types of interactions.*

Being able to provide students with multiple webpages to use and view as a class can certainly help students shift roles between writer, reader, and editor throughout the semester as well as providing them with multiple opportunities to redraft and explain their ideas in detail as they elaborate on information that they gain through their peers reading and editing of their work. A final point Dillenbourg (2000) makes about virtual learning environments, which also applies to wiki use, is that "increasing flexibility is often more crucial than decreasing distance" (p.28). That is to say, it is important for me as a writing teaching to give my students the ability to not only edit their own writing, but to provide an online way to continuously monitor their writing (something that would prove particularly important during emergency remote teaching ERT).

Using a university LMS-based wiki if one is available from your institution, also ensures that student work can be maintained on a secure server from what learners might consider a trusted site. Relying on my university's LMS for most of my instructional provision has enabled me to maintain a record of most of my students' writing for the classes that I have taught, as well as securely maintain a record of instruction in case any issues might later arise.

ERT Use of the University LMS-based Wiki

In February of 2020 many universities in Seoul began to implement or consider a shift to emergency remote teaching (Yonhap News, 2020), which was due to a dramatic rise in COVID-19 cases and based on Ministry of Education recommendations. As Hodges, et al. (2020) point out though, "well-planned online learning experiences are meaningfully different from courses offered online in response to a crisis or disaster," (¶1) and the speed that ERT was rolled out across the globe was "… unprecedented and staggering" (¶3) and also one that "in contrast to experiences that are planned from the beginning and designed to be online … a temporary shift of instructional delivery to an alternate delivery mode due to crisis circumstances" (¶14). In such light, many educators were given little time to decide how to best accommodate their teaching goals using only online platforms. The following details how I utilized the use of my university LMS-based wiki during ERT.

The university LMS-based wiki through my institution, like all others, allows for web page creation and using links to wiki webpages from each of those pages, and for editing via a WYSIWYG (what you see is what you get) interface. The wiki created for the writing classes that I taught allowed every student to view every page within it, and to edit every page. A useful tool to keep track of wiki changes is the edit history, and being able to revert to previous versions of wiki pages from here may at times be required. This is typically the easy option to address any accidental student deletions. It is also a way to revert a page if a student edits the page in their native language instead of English, and this may occur if they have auto-translate turned on in their browser when accessing the wiki.

I have found that by providing each student with their own wiki page helps to prevent any issues that a troublemaker may decide to create while also providing everyone with their own personal online space. During writing classes students can then add additional pages to their own wiki page, as they develop their writing throughout the semester, and as different topics/activities become the focus. To minimize student frustration with wiki use and to facilitate their speedier use of the technology, I created the wiki pages for each student instead of instructing them on how to make their own.

The Writing Tasks

Student learning goals for the writing classes using the LMS-based wiki were those of developing paragraph writing, and multiple paragraph compositions, while collaborating with others so that they could learn from each other. The first task students needed to perform was the editing of the same wiki page, adding their introductory paragraph to it. The next task involved a topic that would have the students write a paragraph about a unique business idea, with me creating a link to another wiki page for all students to then edit for this purpose. The intent here was to have students easily read each other's work and to ensure that they were all able to provide an original idea. After this was complete, every student was given access to their own wiki page. I then added a link to another empty page on each student's wiki page. On their own new wiki page, I added their introduction and business idea so that they could then access the topic here instead of returning to the common workspace pages.

For students to work together, read each other's writing, and then learn from each other and develop their own ideas further as they edit their work, a survey project was then conducted. Each student was given a wiki page to create a survey about their unique business idea. Once created, every student's survey page was then linked to the main class page and every student had to answer the survey of all other learners by leaving a feedback comment at the bottom of that wiki page. After every student completed the activity, students were then directed to write a paragraph about the comments other students left for them as responses to their survey.

Once these writing assignments were complete, students were instructed to review all of their writing and then using a new teacher created link, add a three paragraph 'business report' to the page. This would detail their business idea, the responses to their survey, and a discussion of those responses.

An additional topic, to help facilitate the creative writing process, incorporated the use of various songs that were taught throughout semester and placed on the LMS via video. The wiki writing assignments surrounding this additional topic then involved students writing a self-reflection about these songs and selecting lyrics that had meaning to them. Learners then had to write a paragraph about each song taught and write their self-reflection paragraphs on their own wiki page.

Conclusion

Ultimately, the university LMS-based wiki helped me to effectively allow students to reach the assigned writing goals of the EFL writing classes being taught while dealing with ERT. Further, by using the university LMS-based wiki instead of a commercial wiki I was able to better centralize all my teaching resources for ease of student access and usability. I was also able to maintain records of student work in a secure location on the university server for archiving purposes. Interesting to note, end of semester student feedback indicated that some learners found the wiki the most memorable online experience of their 2020 learning experience.

References

Cary, M. (2020). esln312. Retrieved from http://esln312.pbworks.com

Dillenbourg, P. (2000). Workshop on virtual learning environments. In *EUN Conference 2000: Learning in the New Millennium: Building Education Strategies for Schools*, (1-130).

Hodges, C., Moore, S., Lockee, B., Trust, T., & Bond, A. (2020, March 27). The Difference Between Emergency Remote Teaching and Online Learning. *EDUCAUSE Review*. https://er.educause.edu/articles/2020/3/the-difference-between-emergency-remote-teaching-and-online-learning?fbclid=IwAR22ju2xP2SBkCW9LVQf5P2cEdnbhmX7VbsC8VfbIQoTi805--gI_S4AFmE#:~:text=In%20contrast%20to%20experiences%20that,mode%20due%20to%20crisis%20circumstances

Richardson, W. (2009). *Blogs, wikis, podcasts, and other powerful web tools for Classrooms*, (2nd ed.). Corwin Press.

Yonhap News. (2020, February, 29). Universities in Seoul Shift to Online Classes amid Virus Fears. *Yonhap News Agency*. https://en.yna.co.kr/view/AEN20200228008800315

8. Evolving Identities and Teacher-Student Relationships in the Midst of COVID-19: Teacher Notes

Valentin Tassev
Woosong University

Abstract

The COVID-19 global crisis has affected multiple industries worldwide and has changed the nature and course of human interactions. It has also changed education at all levels, the nature of how we learn and, more importantly, the nature of teacher-student relationships. Taking the latter into account, this exploratory study provides, from the teacher perspective, an examination of classroom observations regarding the nature of teacher-student relationships and learning dynamics as they evolved in an emergency remote teaching class over the span of one academic semester. The teacher argues that this form of online learning, among those not normally expected to participate in it, has helped such students develop new personal, learning, and professional identities in the learning process. In the teacher's eyes, such online learning is seen as a liberating force, which has helped these students perform in new social roles, communicate their opinions more freely than before, exercise new opportunities for academic development and engage with the language that they are learning on a more personalized, intimate, and self-driven level.

---

[*] An expanded version of this work is currently in press, and will appear as: Tassev, V. (2021). Online teacher-student interactions. Diary reflections of an 'old-school' teacher. *The English Connection, 25 (1)*, 16-18.

The Issues at Hand

Throughout the Spring 2020 semester, I taught students from Fuyang Normal University (FNU) in the People's Republic of China who were later supposed to come to the Republic of Korea and complete their education at Woosong University (WSU) as part of a mutual exchange agreement/partnership between FNU and WSU. Due to the COVID 19 global crisis, I could not go to teach the FNU classes face-to-face as initially planned, so these were taught entirely online utilizing in emergency remote teaching (ERT) protocols.

ERT was, in fact, the biggest challenge I was confronted with that semester. I had never taught online prior to the Spring 2020 semester. This practice did not only confront me with completely changing the nature of my teaching methodology, but it also confronted me with having to perform differently as a teacher when using format of teaching. Prior to this experience, I had always been used to being a teacher in the very old fashion sense of the word, whereby I would stand in front of the students and have real-time communication with them, which would largely determine the nature of our relationships and how we perceive one another.

During the Spring 2020 semester, there was no visual contact between myself and my students at all, only audio contact. As teaching online was something new to me and supposedly also the students, I thought it would be wiser to create a more relaxed environment for both the students and I by using the lack of visual contact, at least for a while. Eventually, this practice lasted for the whole semester and we never did see the faces of one another.

In my opinion, this practice resulted in numerous positive effects that I had not envisaged before, which will be discussed shortly. Now though, it should be mentioned that from the outset that this chapter is primarily based on teacher personal observations of the learning process and my communication with students online and, as such, it should be regarded rather as a reflective piece. That said, however, by approaching the piece in this manner it serves to provide the grounds for further research work that can allow for analysis of the impact of online teaching on students' learning outcomes, students' learning identities and teachers' professional identities.

The Online Curriculum

As to the curriculum utilized with the class throughout the semester, the online curriculum ended up being mostly a listening and speaking style curriculum. There was a large number of listening tasks taken from a variety of sources aimed at improving students' listening and comprehension skills. The speaking tasks involved mostly included presentations in groups and individually, as well as providing short individual answers to teacher/group questions. The speaking tasks mostly served the purpose of letting students practice their persuasive speaking skills.

It should be noted here that the teacher planned the curriculum on an ongoing basis, depending on how well the students were coping with the material. Again, due to the COVID-19 crisis, the teacher could not rely on his initial intentions of how and what to teach, in the event that the teacher could have travelled to the People's Republic of China to teach the students in-person.

Implications of Online Learning on Student's Identities and Personas

In the teacher's eyes, the online mode of communication could be regarded as a liberating force as it enabled learners to express their views and opinions freely without the fear of being assessed as right or wrong or having to convey a certain image to the teacher and fellow classmates as a means of seeking approval as in a usual classroom setting. The lack of physical and visual contact seemed to give students a sense of freedom to portray an image of themselves. This image appeared more personalized and driven by the students' genuine desire to participate in the learning forum and perform their roles as learners. Doing so in a way in which they envision engaging in learning rather than being subject to the learning roles pre-assigned by the teacher, the institution or school administrators as is usually the case in a traditional offline setting.

From the students' perspectives, this new line of communication provided them with a series of opportunities to project new identities in the learning process and identify with new roles in this new medium of interactions. Having said that, some students did share that they felt more relaxed to express their opinions being learners in this new forum. Other students shared that they were enabled to communicate their emotions and attitudes in a sincerer manner. Another student expressed the view that the online mode of teaching helped reduce the hierarchical order that would usually exist among students as in a traditional classroom setting.

Here are a few of the opinions that students shared:

> *"... online courses force us to speak English ... on the contrary, face-to-face teaching will make us even more shy."*
> *"I can speak what I want to speak, and don't worry about anybody ... You can have a discussion on a topic everyone is interested in, and everyone should express their own unique opinions."*
> *"I just need to say what I want to say and don't care about others."*

Implications of Online Learning on the Relationships among Teacher and Students

Online learning also had huge implications on the teacher–student relationship(s). In the teacher's understanding, this new mode of communication resulted in building higher levels of mutual trust between the teacher and students. It also helped to create a more positive atmosphere amongst students and the teacher, driven by the common desire to learn from each other and maximize one's learning potential, including that of the teacher in my opinion. For example, teacher and students could tell jokes to one another, behave spontaneously and unpredictably, change, swap and adopt new roles, all depending on any emergent issues at stake in the online sessions and what the lesson(s) evolved into.

With the lack of visual contact and the removal of the barriers of time and space, students were enabled, exposing new identities of themselves, performing new social roles and revealing new personas. Furthermore, they were not worried about how they would be perceived by their teacher and their fellow classmates and, as a result, communicated their viewpoints with joy and a sense of confidence, knowing that their opinions would be heard and acknowledged. Students' levels of confidence also improved largely throughout the semester as they developed these new identities in the process of learning.

Here are a few opinions that students shared:

> *"In online classes, I don't need to see anyone's face or attitude, so I will feel relaxed and comfortable. It makes me more eager to answer all the questions."*
>
> *"Online classes can also improve our confidence."*
>
> *"In online classes, we can enhance the relationship among teacher and students through one-to-one communication. In my opinion, online learning can better promote the relationship between teachers and students. When we have doubts, we can communicate with teachers through the internet anytime and anywhere. It is more timely than traditional face-to-face teaching."*

It was also surprising to see the extent to which the teacher started developing associations, images, and perceptions of students' identities and personas through this line of online communication. For example, students' profile pictures, English names and use of emoticons conveyed certain meanings, and these were reflected and were associated with their own aspirations and engagements with learning the foreign language. Thus, quite often, students would choose English names of foreign celebrities and people they admire, or somehow identify with. Students wanted to be associated with those people in the virtual world and they wanted to be perceived as such by their teacher and the other students too.

Concluding Thoughts

Although a brief exploration, all the findings described here are based upon the teacher's observation of the nature and course of his interactions with students and the process of learning which took place in a single semester with a single class. This chapter, thus, should be regarded only as a departure point into the quest of making further inquiries surrounding the role of online learning in the development of new learning and professional identities, concerning teacher and students, respectively.

What is equally important is perhaps how students feel at the end of a course and what their own impressions are of the course, their own learning and, last but not least, their teacher. These are all, at least from my perspective, variables that largely define the success of a course and any associated learning outcomes.

Has student learning been productive and efficient? Have their own learning expectations and learning goals been successfully met? Have they become more responsible and autonomous learners, after all? Have their epistemological beliefs about learning remained the same, or have they changed dramatically? Have students built a new relationship with the language? Emerging, then, the most fundamental question: does the language learning process help the learner expand their personal identity and broaden their perspectives and horizons in various ways? At this stage, the answers to most of these questions would prove highly ambivalent and contrasting since online learning still proves new to many forced to participate in it.

As a response to some of these questions, at least, some students from the course shared that they had become more confident in English. Other students stated that they had become more willing to explore the language while others shared that they had built new interests in learning languages and in learning *per se*, as a result of participating in this style of class, with a few stating that they would like to continue studying online. Interestingly too, a few also even went so far as to say that they had decided to become English language teachers, a job that they had never imagined they would ever consider, not to mention perform and do for a living. These final confessions alone could be a steppingstone into their exploration of the English language and largely a new exploration of self not previously conceivable.

Bibliography

Cunningham, G. (2020, October 19). *Term 4-online learning in a Covid Environment: An authentic learning experience?* https://www.barker.college/head-of-barker-college-blog/2020/term-4/online-learning-in-a-covid-environment-an-authentic-learning-experience

Gao, L. & Zhang, L. (2020, September 15). *Teacher learning in difficult times: Examining foreign language teachers' cognitions about online teaching to tide over COVID-19.* https://www.frontiersin.org/articles/10.3389/fpsyg.2020.54965 3/full

Morris, S. (2020, April 17). *A pedagogy of transformation for times of crisis.* https://oeb.global/oeb-insights/a-pedagogy-of-transformation-for-times-of-crisis

Poulton, P. & Yoo, R. (2020, July 1). *Renegotiating teacher identities: Reflections on student wellbeing and online learning during COVID-19.* https://www.bera.ac.uk/blog/renegotiating-teacher-identities-reflections-on-student-wellbeing-and-online-learning-during-covid-19

Spencer, G. (2020, June 17). *Schools after COVID-19: From a teaching culture to a learning culture.* https://news.microsoft.com/apac/features/technology-in-schools-from-a-teaching-culture-to-a-learning-culture

Yulandari, E. (2020). English students' perception about daring learning while quarantine: A qualitative case study. *JOLLT Journal of Languages and Language Teaching, 8*(3), 315-322.

Appendix A: Symposium Schedule

SYMPOSIUM SCHEDULE – 일정	
10:00	**Welcoming Ceremony – 환영식**
10:10	**Plenary Speaker – 총회 연사** Building successful on-demand video courses *Wayne Finley*
11:00	The role of vocabulary in needs analysis *Marina Dodigovic*
11:30	Time-saving dynamic rubrics for effective online feedback and scoring *Jan Mathys de Beer*
12:00	Integrated approaches using student generated content *Andrew Aguiar and Nicole Shiosaki*
12:50	Teaching in a time of crisis and the opportunities to inspire social activism *Cyril Reyes*
13:40	**Keynote – 기조연설** Working memory strategy efficacy for the Pearson Test of English Academic speaking *Miranda Wu*
14:30	**Closing Speaker - 클로징 연사** The future of MA(TESOL) online *James Robinson, St. Cloud State University*
15:00	**Closing Ceremony – 폐회식** *Prize draw and TESOL-MALL program final Q&A*

SYNCHRONOUS SESSIONS – 동시에 진행되는 세션

Symposium Asynchronous Sessions – 동시 진행되지 않는 심포지엄 세션

VIRTUAL PRESENTATIONS — *https://tesolmall.weebly.com/presentations-2021*
The three 'tenses' of Education: Past (imperfect), present, and future (indefinite) *Dawn Edgecome*
Communicating with Korean students – Crossing the cultural barrier (preconceptions and cultural differences) *Retha Choi*
Group work: Its effectiveness on learning the English Language among the students of Korea University of Media Arts *Carmela Quiatchon*
A multi-label question tagging tool for item classification in question repositories *Irada Gezalova and Arthur Ganeev*
An analysis of a university LMS-based wiki for English writing during emergency remote teaching *Michael Cary*
Evolving identities and teacher-student relationships in the midst of COVID-19: Teacher notes *Valentin Tassev*

ASYNCHRONOUS SESSIONS – 동시에 진행되지 않는 세션

Appendix B: Symposium Abstracts

Synchronous Sessions – Zoom Presentations

Talk 1:
Plenary
Building Successful On-Demand Video Courses
Wayne Finley, Korea Polytechnic University

Talk 2
The Role of Vocabulary in Needs Analysis
Marina Dodigovic, University of la Rioja

Talk 3
Time-Saving Dynamic Rubrics for Effective Online Feedback and Scoring
Jan Mathys de Beer, Woosong University

Talk 4
A New Era for English Classes: Exploring the Concept of Social Media Marketing Activities and English Communication Skills
Andrew Aguiar, Gyeongsang National University
Nicole Shiosaki, Gyeongsang National University

Talk 5
Defense of social justice in education
Cyril Reyes

Talk 6:
Keynote
Working Memory Strategy Efficacy for the Pearson Test of English Academic Speaking
Miranda Wu

Talk 7:
Closing
The future of MA(TESOL) online
James Robinson

Talk 1: Plenary

Building Successful On-Demand Video Courses

Wayne Finley, Korea Polytechnic University

The coronavirus pandemic of 2020 thrust a lot of teachers into the world of online teaching, but teaching online is nothing new. Massive open online courses (MOOCs) through providers like Udemy and Coursera have proven to be extremely popular. As of today, Udemy has more than 40 million learners, 50,000 instructors and over 30 million minutes of content. The popularity of MOOCs offers a world of opportunity for teachers. Successful on-demand video courses reach thousands of students all over the globe and can generate a reliable source of passive income.

In this presentation, we will cover the basics of everything a teacher needs to build courses for commercial MOOC providers like Udemy. From acquiring the right equipment, structuring the curriculum, creating engaging content, through to editing of the videos and the means of launching a successful marketing campaign for the course. You will leave this presentation with all the basics, and what's more, you will also receive valuable tips and advice to give your courses the upper hand in such a competitive environment. MOOCs are here and they are here to stay. Join us to get started!

Talk 2

The Role of Vocabulary in Needs Analysis
Marina Dodigovic, University of la Rojia

Understanding the needs of second or foreign language (L2) learners is essential in the process of both planning and delivering L2 lessons. Vocabulary seems to be particularly underrepresented in needs analysis. Needs analysis is the kind of investigation "curriculum developers use to identify the gap between what learners already know and what they need to know in order to study or work in their specific target environments" (Basturkmen, 2005, p. 15). Failing to determine which vocabulary the students already know and what might be the realistic vocabulary targets for their classes is likely to result in failure to make progress in the target language, an outcome unfortunately too often observed in foreign language settings. Similarly, failing to examine the extent to which textbook vocabulary addresses the needs of students, more often than not, results in the absence of learning. Finally, vocabulary learning strategies are frequently taken for granted, leaving the students ill equipped for the task. This talk will share the experiences regarding the above three variables gathered in the context of the pandemic precipitated online English classes and make recommendations for the post-pandemic era.

Talk 3

Time-Saving Dynamic Rubrics for Effective Online Feedback and Scoring

Jan Mathys de Beer, Woosong University

There are many advantages to online language teaching, but one of the great disadvantages is not being able to easily provide personalized feedback to students so they can improve in the areas where they are struggling. This becomes a particularly difficult task with large class sizes or when scheduled with many classes to teach. Yet, electronic dynamic rubrics can prove to be time-saving and effective for providing both constructive feedback and in providing ways to connect your feedback to the marks of a student. Getting the balance right between coaching students' language learning and showing them how they have improved is not an easy task. This talk provides the reader with practical examples to develop their own time-saving, effective dynamic rubrics for online, hybrid, and traditional classroom contexts.

Talk 4

Integrated Approaches Using Student Generated Content
Andrew Aguiar, Gyeongsang National University
Nicole Shiosaki, Gyeongsang National University

The pandemic emerging in 2020 has expanded online teaching methods through technological integration. One teaching approach that has benefited from online class provision is the use of student generated content. Student generated content allows language learners to interact with content made by other language learners. As all students require a device with internet access when teaching online, interacting with student generated content is much easier than in face-to-face contexts because students can conveniently interact through applications, such as Flipgrid. This gives students a chance to hear non-standard English, gives students ownership over their language learning and gives students a chance to interact with their peers in different ways. In order to gain the most from student generated content, the students' original outputs can be used as input for other students who utilize it to develop the next output in a student generated integrated skills approach. This presentation illustrates specific examples of activities and projects centered around using Flipgrid to create student generated content for learners to interact with while integrating multiple language skills into their development of student generated content. Post-pandemic, the methods used to develop an online student generated integrated approach can be worthwhile implementing from within the face-to-face classroom.

Talk 5

Defense of Social Justice in Education

Cyril Reyes, Wosoong University

In response to the recent COVID-19 pandemic and social and political discord, I clarify the moral and political justification for applying social justice ideas in education, by defining the moral obligation of educators in regard to social and political issues today. The need for clarification on this subject derives from the conflation of social justice and political correctness, which reduces the moral substance of social activism to censorship and cultural policing. This paper then, is not only a defense of social justice in education but provides a conceptual framework to separate the moral duty from the combative nature of political discourse. This conceptual framework is discussed through three specific positions: 1) a strong belief in social justice, 2) that of ambivalence, and 3) that of being uncomfortable with politics. Each of these positions is then defined by their specific political and non-political stances along with their respective moral justifications and what this means for those teachers that may adhere to such perspectives.

Talk 6: Keynote

Working Memory Strategy Efficacy for the Pearson Test of English Academic Speaking

Miranda Wu, Huaihua University

In the computer-based Pearson Test of English, Academic (PTEA), test-takers and instructors are usually eager to understand how the reporting algorithm is based on the enabling skills (ES) and communicative skills (CS) scores shown on test reports. Undoubtedly, their interest in investigating the algorithm are driven by endeavoring to develop strategies to improve their speaking score in the test. This presentation examines aspects of how to obtain better performance in this test, analyzing 214 score reports collected from 107 participants over a three-year longitudinal experiment exploring strategies and cognitive factors that influence performance. We test efficacy of working memory (WM) by developing latent constructs for tasks. Findings show that WM strategies can explain significant variance in complexity, accuracy and fluency (CAF) in both experiments and in actual tests. Fluency, reflected by articulation speed, breakdowns and repair, is the predominant component here because the use of fluency-oriented strategies can improve speaking performance rapidly and lead to lexical complexity and phonological accuracy transfer. Cognitive factors such as response latency, speed fluency, attention, confidence and target score as motivation are significant for the variance. Findings indicate awareness of mapping learners' meta-cognition with WM strategies during instruction to optimize test outcome, and this has implications for tutors assisting students in passing the speaking component of the PTEA.

Talk 7: Closing Speaker

The Future of MA(TESOL) Online

James Robinson, St. Cloud State University

This short session will present on how universities will need to address the dilemma in higher education moving forward, and how this impacts those who wish to undertake an MA(TESOL). The importance of graduate qualifications, and TESOL specializations are discussed, and a unique avenue for dual degree completion is provided.

Asynchronous Sessions

Talk 8	**The Three 'Tenses' of Education: Past (Imperfect), Present, and Future (Indefinite)**

Dawn Edgecome
Woosong Information College

Talk 9	**Communicating with Students in the Korean Classroom – Crossing the Cultural Barrier (Preconceptions and Cultural Differences)**

Retha Choi
Woosong Information College

Talk 10	**Group Work: Its Effects on Learning the English Language among the Students of Korea University of Media Arts**

Carmela Quiatchon, Woosong University

Talk 11	**A Multi-Level Question Tagging Tool for Item Classification in Question Repositories**

Irada Gezaalova, Woosong University
Arthur Ganeev, Samsung SDI

Talk 12	**An Analysis of a University LMS-Based Wiki for English Writing During Emergency Remote Teaching**

Michael Cary
Kyeonggi University – Suwon Campus

Talk 13	**Reimaging Teaching: The Future of Language and Education. What do you need in a Post COVID Society to Keep your Sanity and Your Job?**

Valentin Tassev
Woosong University

Talk 8

The Three 'Tenses' of Education: Past (Imperfect), Present, and Future (Indefinite)

Dawn Edgecome, Woosong University

Education has crossed the Rubicon in 2020. What we thought we knew is no longer relevant and in the struggle to stay relevant, we have lost many aspects of our profession and gained many more. This presentation will focus on the three 'tenses' of education. It will give a brief history of education, dividing it into the past: education prior to 1717, the present: education from 1717-2020, and the future: 2021 onwards. It will discuss what we knew, what we thought we knew, and what we definitely don't know. The main focus of the discussion will be on what we have learned from the chaos that was 2020, and how we can begin to apply new ideas and progressive technology, and how to handle the 'new' students. Education has not only changed from a teacher's perspective, but also from that of the student. As teachers, we may tend to forget that we were not the only ones who were severely disrupted during this pandemic. Our students had to learn an entirely new method of schooling, and although the majority of our students are proficient in the use of technology, many of us may have expected so much more of them. It is possibly one of the most dramatic changes that have taken place in education in our lifetime, and moving forward we need to be ready to face the challenges to come.

Talk 9

Communicating with Students in the Korean Classroom – Crossing the Cultural Barrier (Preconceptions and Cultural Differences)

Retha Choi, Woosong University

There are a couple of important questions that can be raised when thinking about communicating with English language students in the Republic of Korea (hereafter Korea). To begin with, why is it important to communicate clearly between the teacher and these students? Secondly, what kind of cultural and permanent misunderstandings can occur between the teacher and these students? Clear communication is required in order to provide a great teaching experience for students as miscommunication may occur due to an inappropriate use of verbal and non-verbal cues which can then lead to cultural misunderstandings. This may then result in the student becoming anxious and consciously or subconsciously then not responding to the teacher. Educators should also limit their use of jargon, idioms, sarcasm, or academic words, as these might confuse uninformed students. Negative biases and cultural differences between teachers and students are also considered in classroom communication in this talk. Here, students may have separate ways of learning that are at odds to the teacher's learning ideals and biases, which can then lead to poor communication through verbal cues, preconceptions, and cultural differences. The first step for teachers is to acknowledge these problems and take a few simple steps to reduce them. This can be achieved by establishing a good rapport, showing empathy, and by being aware of verbal and nonverbal cues. Also, be aware of any use of confusing or intimidating language and actions until students get used to your teaching style. As well, use open-ended questions to let students know that care is being given for their feedback. This talk will also explore these issues and expand on ways to implement them in the classroom through a flipped classroom pedagogical approach and through the author's experiences of teaching in Korea both before and during the COVID-19 pandemic. Some implications for post-pandemic teaching going forward emerge.

Talk 10

Group Work: Its Effects on Learning the English Language among the Students of Korea University of Media Arts

Carmela Quiatchon, Woosong University

Learning English has been an in-demand skill among Koreans at all school levels. Most of Korean parents would rather their child or children learn the English language at an early age since English increases the chances of getting a good job within South Korea or for finding a job abroad. It is also the language of international communication, the media, and the internet. Moreover, learning the language can increase confidence and provide a sense of personal achievement in the learner. In line with this, this study focuses on the effectiveness of group work in learning the English language among the students of Korea University of Media Arts. The university students have been learning the English language for many years. They are exposed to the said language and most of these respondents have a desire to learn English since they will be needing the language to go abroad and to be globally competitive. The researcher will use a demographic survey, with a Likert-type scale. Furthermore, respondents will be asked about their personal information, including questions relating to their preference of either learning the English language on their own or with a group, and how often they study the language. Results relating to the effectiveness of group work in learning English among these learners are presented.

Talk 11

A Multi-Label Question Tagging Tool for Item Classification in Question Repositories

Irada Gezalova, Woosong University
Arthur Ganeev, Samsung SDI

Various types of assessments require the development of question papers from teachers or educators. This process could be tedious and time-consuming, moreover the developer has to be an expert at question paper composing. Nowadays, a variety of applications and tools exist that can assist teachers in the process of question paper development. Mostly, these assistant tools form questions from questions repositories (QR) and could be semi-automated or automated. Semi-automated tools require human support, while automated ones can produce questions paper without any additional assistance. In spite of the multiplicity of the existence of automated applications and tools, they still have limitations. Mast of the existing projects of Automatic Generation of Question Papers' (AGQP) instruments focus on four tags: topic (content), question type, cognitive level, and difficulty level. When it comes to the first tag, development of topic (content) documents, researchers classify QR by using one content tag for one question (multi-class classification). Whereas the efficiency of a tool depends on its ability to arrange multiple content tags, in other words to allow multi-label classification. As such, in this project we are going to implement a multi-label classification algorithm by teaching it using QR acquired from theenglish.stackexchange.com forum. This forum contains numerous Q&A posts that can allow for teaching the algorithm precisely based on a wide range of input data. Additionally, the tool developed is going to be posted on github.com, and can be used freely as a QR multi-label tool, or in future research and/or development projects. Moreover, the obtained multiple tagged QR can be used by teachers for question paper generation.

Talk 12

An Analysis of a University LMS-based Wiki for English Writing during Emergency Remote Teaching

Michael Cary,
Kyonggi University – Suwon Campus

This presentation will discuss the basic principles of wikis and how to use one in an English writing class. Examples of a commercial wiki are examined and compared to a university learner management system (LMS) wiki. Everything possible with the university LMS wiki will be shown, with student examples for each activity highlighting how learners can interact with each other using it. The presentation will then conclude by detailing how assessments can be undertaken while accounting for the limitations of the LMS wiki.

Talk 13

Evolving Identities and Teacher-Student Relationships in the Midst of COVID-19: Teacher Notes

Valentin Tassev, Woosong University

The COVID-19 global crisis has affected multiple industries worldwide and has changed the nature and course of human interactions. It has also changed education at all levels, the nature of how we learn and, more importantly, the nature of teacher-student relationships. Taking the latter into account, this study provides, from the teacher perspective, an examination of classroom observations regarding the nature of teacher-student relationships and learning dynamics as they evolved in emergency remote teaching classes over the span of one academic semester. The teacher argues that this form of online learning, among those not normally expected to participate in it, has helped such students develop new personal, learning, and professional identities in the learning process. In the teacher's eyes, such online learning is seen as a liberating force, which has helped these students perform in new social roles, communicate their opinions more freely than before, exercise new opportunities for academic development and engage with the language that they are learning on a more personalized, intimate, and self-driven level.

Appendix C: Presenter Biographies

Presenter Biographies in Presentation Order

Wayne Finley is a teacher, teacher trainer and is the current Korea TESOL Publicity Chair. He first arrived on Korean shores to teach children, but since 2012 has primarily taught university students. Among his achievements are a TEDx talk in 2018 and several awards for his teaching and volunteering. In his free time, he loves to create video content and in 2019 he started building video courses. As of today, his English teaching and teacher training Udemy courses have proved popular: tens of thousands of enrollments and 5-star ratings.

Marina Dodigovic is an honorary professor of English and TESOL at the University of la Rioja. She has taught in MA TESOL programs internationally and conducted relevant research, which is documented in a number of books and peer reviewed journal articles.

Jan Mathys de Beer has many years' experience in education, research, and publishing, with degrees in philosophy, religion, ethics, psychology, and applied education. He has been an Assistant-Professor at Woosong University, in the republic of Korea, since 2017 where he teaches English and Research and & Writing courses. Until the pandemic in 2020, he acted as research coordinator.

Andrew Aguiar teaches at Gyeongsang National University. He is the head of the School of Language Education curriculum committee (SLECC) and is one of the organizers of the university's monthly online workshops. He is a graduate of Woosong University's TESOL-MALL program.

Nicole Shiosaki is currently teaching at Gyeongsang National University. She is secretary of the School of Language Education curriculum committee (SLECC) and is one of the organizers of the university's monthly online workshops. She is also a graduate of Woosong University's TESOL-MALL program.

Cyril Reyes is an Assistant Professor at Woosong University and a regular contributor to Korea TESOL's publicity efforts.

Miranda Wu (Wu Yang) is a Business English Lecturer at the Huaihua University in the People's Republic of China. She earned her PhD at Woosong University in the Republic of Korea and her master's degree from the Foreign Linguistics and Applied Linguistics department of Central South University. She also provides Pearson Test of English Academic (PTEA) online sessions and teacher education at the Alpaca PTEA research center where she currently serves as a research fellow. Currently serving on the editorial board of Computer Assisted Language Learning, an international SSCI level journal, her principal research interests revolve around instructional technology, artificial intelligence in linguistics, and digital language learning. She has published a number of books, including the *Pearson Test of English Academic Introduction, Strategies and Answers* and *Language Learning with Artificial Intelligence in the Fourth Industrial Revolution Era*.

James Robinson is Head of the TESOL program at and a professor in the Department of English at St. Cloud State University in Minnesota, USA. He has widely published in his field of expertise. His research areas include the teaching of English as a second language, computer assisted language learning and digital literacy, second language acquisition, second language research methods, and second language teaching methods.

Dawn *Edgecome* is an Assistant Professor at Woosong Information College, assigned to the Sol International School of Culinary Arts and Pastry. She has been teaching for 26 years and has worked in South Korea for 5 years. She has been teaching at Woosong Information College since 2017. Dawn has taught students from Kindergarten, to adults and has taught a variety of subjects. Her focus, however, has always been on English. She has taught English as a Home Language, Foreign Language, First Additional Language and Second Additional Language. Her teaching career started in South Africa, where she taught in Primary Schools and High Schools. She received her B.A. Degree from the University of Pretoria, in 1988, her PGCE (cum laude) from the University of Johannesburg in 2011, and a post-graduate degree (B.Ed. Hon.) in School Management and Curriculum Development from the University of South Africa in 2017.

Retha Choi is an Assistant Professor at Woosong Information College in the Nursing Department, teaching English for specific purposes (ESP) courses. She holds a Master of Arts from the TESOL-MALL graduate program at Woosong University, and a graduate of the Bachelor of Social Work, Walla Walla University, Washington. She has volunteered as an academic advisor at HOPE- a registered non-profit NGO based in Seoul, and an organization that provides free English language courses for disadvantaged families and children (www.alwayshope.or.kr). She has lived and worked in Korea for 25 years, and maintains 19 years of teaching experience across three universities in Daejeon. She enjoys being creative and developing curriculum materials for all of her classes.

Carmela Quiatchon holds a Bachelor of Arts (majoring in English). Currently, she is pursuing her M.A. degree at Woosong University and is working as an English instructor in Sejong City, South Korea.

Irada Gezalova is post graduate student of TESOL MALL department at Woosong University, with her main interests that of the application of artificial intelligence in education.

Arthur Ganeev, PhD is a principle engineer at Samsung SDI and his main interests lay in data mining and machine learning.

Michael Cary is an Assistant Professor at Kyonggi University – Suwon Campus. He has been teaching in the Republic of Korea at the university level since 2010. He began teaching in 2004 and has taught a wide range of students from pre-Kindergarten to post-doctoral from all over the world, both in the Republic of Korea and in the United States of America. He received his B.S. and M.A. from Eastern Michigan University. His research focuses on how best to use wikis in language classrooms, and he has globally presented and published on this topic.

Valentin Tassev is an Assistant Professor at Woosong University and is pursuing his M.A. degree through the Woosong University TESOL-MALL graduate program.

Appendix D: Symposium Recognition and Development

Plenary
Building successful on-demand video courses.
Wayne Finley.

Keynote
Working memory strategy efficacy for the Pearson Academic Test
of English speaking.
Miranda Wu.

Symposium Organization

David Kent.

Symposium Website

David Kent.

Symposium Advertising

David Kent.
KOTESOL DCC.

Symposium Program Book

David Kent.

Symposium Proceedings

David Kent.

Symposium Chair

David Kent.

Zoom Session Moderator

Mark Love.

About the Book

As teachers taught through the global pandemic that began in Asia during the later months of 2019 and has since gripped the world, they have employed technology and their training to lead educational change. They have achieved this by riding the wave of a paradigm shift for the mainstream provision of education, predominantly by rising to the challenge of adapting to and delivering emergency remote teaching. Changes moving forward will likely continue with the ever-increasing digitalization of education, the hybridization of education on return to the classroom, and the possible increase of blended and distance learning offerings institution-wide (along with an increasing need to develop asynchronous and synchronous online and offline learning activities and opportunities for learners).

This book puts forth a snapshot of how English as a foreign language (EFL) teachers in the Republic of Korea professionally handled the 'COVID crisis', and how they now see their craft, their administrative, teaching, and learning contexts, as well as how their learners should be educated in not only a post-pandemic, but possibly a COVID endemic world. It is, therefore, an essential read for any educator, student, administrator, or stakeholder involved with the teaching of English to speakers of other languages (TESOL), particularly those who want to understand how pre-service and in-service teachers are honing their teaching craft, and how post-pandemic pedagogy is currently impacting the educational sector.

Books in the
TESOL-MALL/KOTESOL DCC
Symposium Series

The Fourth Industrial Revolution and Education:
Digital Language Learning and Teaching

Reimagining Languaging:
The Future of Teaching and Education

Post-Pandemic Pedagogy:
Tools of the TESOL Trade

About the Editor

David Kent is an Associate Professor in the Endicott College of International Studies at Woosong University in the Republic of Korea. He provides teacher education through the TESOL-MALL graduate program where he currently serves as Head of Department.

David is a long-standing member of the academic community with a principal research focus that revolves around digital language learning. He has been a member of KOTESOL, living and teaching in Korea since 1995.

He has published a number of books, including *Teaching with Technology: Integrating Technology into the TESOL Classroom, Internet in Education: Integrating the Internet into the TESOL Classroom*, and a *TESOL Strategy Guide* series that focuses on the use of specific digital tools for teaching. He has also authored a number of multimedia applications.

Currently, David serves on the editorial board of several journals, and his research articles have been published at the Scopus and SSCI levels in such periodicals as *Teaching English with Technology, The Journal of Asia TEFL*, and the prestigious *Language Learning and Technology*.